The Spiritual Gifts

Understanding for the Great Shift and Beyond

Chariss K. Walker, M.Msc.

Libraries and booksellers interested in stocking The Vision Chronicles series and other books by Chariss K. Walker --

Direct Reseller Application --
https://www.createspace.com/pub/l/createspacedirect.do

For Wholesale and Library Distribution:

Create Space Direct

Attn: Customer Service

4900 Lacross Road

N. Charleston, SC 29406

Fax: (206) 922-5928

Email: info@createspace.com

Website: https://www.createspace.com

Copyright © 2012 Chariss K Walker

All rights reserved under International and Pan-American Copyright Conventions.

ISBN 13: 978-1-469-90320-0
ISBN 10:1-46990-320-2

The Spiritual Gifts

Cover Design by Chariss K Walker
Image: http://i1125.photobucket.com/albums/l598/kicmac/Abstract/abstract-rainbow-.jpg

Disclaimer

Although the author and publisher have made every effort to ensure that the information in this book was correct at press time, the author and publisher do not assume and hereby disclaim any liability to any party for any loss, damage, or disruption caused by errors or omissions, whether such errors or omissions result from negligence, accident, or any other cause. Because of the dynamic nature of the Internet, any Web addresses or links contained in this book may have changed since this publication and may no longer be valid.

The author's intent is to offer information of a general nature that will help you, the reader, in your search for spiritual well-being. The author does not dispense medical advice or prescribe medications of any kind. This book is not intended as a substitute for the medical advice of physicians. The reader should regularly consult a physician in matters relating to his/her health and particularly with respect to any symptoms that may require diagnosis or medical attention.

Table of Contents

Forward..v

Part I – Introduction to Spiritual Gifts 1

Chapter 1 – The Benefit of Spiritual Gifts 3

Chapter 2 – The Importance of Living in the Heart............6

Chapter 3 – The Purpose of Spiritual Gifts.............9

Chapter 4 – Spiritual Gifts Today......................11

Chapter 5 – Evidence of Spiritual Gifts..............15

Chapter 6 – Spiritual Gifts for Now and the Future......20

Part II – The Spiritual Gifts Examined 23

Chapter 7 – Empathic..................................25

Chapter 8 – Creative Force............................31

Chapter 9 – Clairsentient.............................37

Chapter 10 – Clairvoyant..............................43

Chapter 11 – Intuitive................................49

Chapter 12 – Seer.....................................55

Chapter 13 – Reader...................................61

Chapter 14 – Energy Manipulation......................65

Chapter 15 – Medium...................................71

Chapter 16 – Light Bearer.............................77

Chapter 17 – Applied Kinesiology......................83

Chapter 18 – Crossing-Over Departed Spirits 89

Chapter 19 – Instinct..95

Chapter 20 – Dream Interpreter 101

Chapter 21 – Healing 107

Chapter 22 – Faith 113

Chapter 23 – Magnetic Energy 117

Chapter 24 – Sacred Symbols 123

Chapter 25 – Remote Viewing................................... 127

Chapter 26 – Visualization 131

Chapter 27 – Channeling 135

Chapter 28 – Bringing Down the Light 141

Chapter 29 – Bringing Down Energy 147

Chapter 30 – Prayer.. 151

Chapter 31 – Teaching 155

Bonus excerpt from *Chakra Basics*...............................161

About the Author ....…..181

Additional Resources 183

Forward

With clarity of thought and purpose Chariss K. Walker has written a valuable text for readers wanting to understand the nature of spiritual gifts and learn if they possess them. For those who have already been so blessed, the book provides a detailed examination of 24 of the most common, how to master them, and how each is most useful.

Walker emphasizes that, as we are all spiritual beings having a human experience, we all have a propensity toward one or many such metaphysical traits. As I read through the list I thought, "Oh...I have evidence of at least one of the indicators in each category." I'm a writer and ideas are often "channeled" through me from some intangible spirit energy. Creative Force is an innate part of me. My Intuitive instincts tell me when that phone call is coming from someone I have been thinking of, or where the closest parking space is in a sea of cars, or that some unseen hand has moved my car out of the way of a speeding truck that could have plowed me over. These are simplistic and mundane examples, of course. Having true Spiritual Gifts encompass so much more, and mastering your gifts takes devotion, practice, determination, and faith.

Walker gives valuable tools and tips to help you develop whichever gift(s) resonate with you. As with all such things that reap great rewards there is great responsibility. Your gifts are not for channeling the winning lottery numbers or for self-aggrandizement. They are not for you to control. They can only be used with love, for the betterment of mankind. Spiritual gifts cannot be measured by scientific or material observation. They are accepted on faith and are materialized by "living in the heart."

Barbara Roman, Author

Part I

Introduction to Spiritual Gifts

In the following section, we'll discuss important aspects of the spiritual gifts to help further your understanding.

- The benefits of having spiritual gifts
- The importance of living in the heart
- The purpose of spiritual gifts
- Spiritual gifts today
- Evidence of spiritual gifts
- And, spiritual gifts for now and the future

Chapter 1

The Benefits of Spiritual Gifts

The purpose of this book is to explain the spiritual gifts and their benefit to mankind during and after the great shift of 2012. A simple explanation is that these gifts are from the Spirit of All; they are gifts from the Father/Mother consciousness of All. The bible and other texts refer to them as gifts of the Spirit.

Beginning with Chapter Seven, I have left additional pages at the end of each chapter for your notes about each gift, but I also recommend that you have a notebook handy. Listen closely to your heart and notate that which stands out to you.

Just as you have received certain traits from your natural parents' biology, you also received certain traits from your spiritual parents. The traits you received from your natural parents are physical while the traits you receive from your spiritual parents are metaphysical (beyond the physical) or spiritual in nature. After all, you are the children of

God/Universe and it is only natural that His/Her spiritual physiology would be yours as well.

Spiritual gifts are metaphysical because the gifts cannot be measured by scientific or material observation. They are accepted on faith.

Faith is a derivative of love and comes from the actual heart organ itself. If you have worked with the heart organ in thanksgiving and gratitude before selecting this book, then you understand this concept. If you have not worked with the heart organ, then start with the First Step below before you continue reading this book. If you are one of those individuals who can read instructions and follow them immediately as you read, then do it now. Jump into the heart now.

First Step --Living in the heart

Place your right hand over the physical location of the heart. Feel the heartbeat. Find the rhythm of this marvelous organ and listen closely to its tempo. With each beat utter the words, "Thank you." Visualize the blood pushing your gratitude in these two simple words throughout the body as it circulates. Make a conscious choice using your Divine birthright of Free-Will to declare, "It is my desire to live in the heart."

Making the choice is that simple.

Living in the heart means that you are conscious of everything as it pertains to the heart – that all decisions, all thoughts will issue from the heart. Each time that you choose between one thing and another, consciously focus on the heart. Place your hand over the physical location of the heart

The Spiritual Gifts

and center yourself there as a reminder that it is your choice to live in the heart.

The Spiritual Gifts come from the heart and it is from the heart that you will use them successfully. They cannot be used from the third dimension of power and control. They can only be used with love, the God-Consciousness.

Practice the First Step on the previous page until you feel your own personal shift from third to fourth dimension, the shift from fear to love.

Chapter 2

The Importance of Living in the Heart

Currently mankind in general lives in the third dimension, or the ego. All decisions are based in fear, lack, control, separation and other derivatives of fear.

To use the spiritual gifts to their full advantage, it is imperative to shift into the heart or fourth dimension especially now, in 2012 and beyond. In the fourth dimension, all decisions are based in love, compassion, freedom, oneness, empathy and the other derivatives of love.

If we are to save our planet and life for future generations, we must come from a place of love to do so. Love in the key. Love is God. Love is in the heart. God is in the heart of mankind.

It is through love in the fourth dimension that you will create a new reality. The new reality will tear-down the old reality of ego. It will replace the old reality of power and control, the old guard.

Yes, you create your life and reality by your thoughts. Each thought that you have has the potential to manifest into material reality, into physical objects and emotional joy or suffering.

You are the creator of your life!

Currently the thoughts that are manifest in this world are echoes of the third dimension – war, strife, shortage, destruction, greed, separation, and the like which are based in fear.

During the great shift into the fourth dimension of the heart the reality you create will be echoes of love – peace, happiness, plenty, reconstruction, sharing, oneness and the like.

The thoughts you think the most are made manifest by the Universe. Resolve now to think thoughts of love and to create a paradise of love.

It is important to understand this concept because during and after the great shift of 2012 mankind will consciously use his/her psychic abilities to change the world.

You do this now without realizing the implications, without awareness, but later you will have hard evidence of this spiritual law and it's undeniably. For example, perhaps you see a commercial on television that promotes weight-loss. You are interested and buy the product. The product either works or doesn't work because of your belief that it will or won't. Maybe it works for the first 20 pounds but then it stops working. The reason it stops working is due to your belief.

This is the way that every experience is created – whether it is a personal relationship, a job or an idea. You believe and it works. When you stop believing it stops working.

All of it, every experience, is created by your thoughts and beliefs.

Chapter 3

The Purpose of Spiritual Gifts

You have been given spiritual gifts because you are spiritual beings having an earthly experience. It is easy to only realize the body because it is material -- you can see and feel it. But it is your original path to rediscover yourself as spiritual beings.

You are body, mind and soul -- multidimensional. You are the Divine children of God. God is the spirit of all and in all. His/Her spirit is in you and it is this spiritual thread that connects you to the All.

When you work with the heart energy of oneness this becomes a solid reality. Become familiar with this now. Know the love of the heart which is God.

There is a great awakening on the horizon, an awakening to your true self. No more will you see yourself as only human. No more will you feel trapped in powerless situations.

Love conquers all and it is in love that you will be the conquering hero rather than the helpless slave trapped in third dimensional thinking.

Now more than ever it is time to move into the heart dimension. The heart dimension is the fourth dimension. It is a growth process that requires the choice of your personal free-will. The great shift requires mankind to move or shift into the fourth dimension leaving the ego mentality or old guard thinking behind.

The fourth dimension is conscious of the oneness of all. The fourth dimension is the place where love rules. Love seeks goodness and plenty for all. Love sees the oneness in all things and all people. Love understands there is no shortage of anything and freely gives.

Keeping the differences in third and fourth dimension in mind as relating to the old way versus the new way, it is understandable that the shift will not be easy for some. Thankfully the Universe/God has given gifts to make this transition from third to fourth dimension easier.

Do not be afraid of your gifts. Open your heart to receive whatever gifts are yours and begin to work with them now. Become familiar with these gifts so that during the shift and beyond you might have what it takes to help others during their transition as well.

Chapter 4

Spiritual Gifts Today

Many who have spiritual gifts are cast in an unfavorable light in our society. Most professionals prescribe medication for those who are awakening to their spiritual blessings. Since there is little information available about these gifts many struggle on their own to understand the changes in their lives. As a result these gifts are often seen as a curse rather than a blessing.

Spiritual gifts are a blessing. It takes training and persistence to fully understand all things and spiritual gifts are not an exception to that rule. For example, a budding channel begins by first hearing voices. If the channel tells another channel, the two compare similarities and the channel knows he/she is not alone and that the experiences are normal for other channels. However, if the channel does not know another with this same gift, he/she stands a greater chance of being misunderstood and criticized. Well-meaning friends and family might tell the channel that hearing voices is a sign of mental illness. They might suggest she seek counseling.

For example, an Indigo child was tortured by her family for seeing spiritual entities beyond the age when most children stop seeing. The mother and all siblings repeatedly told the child that nothing was there because they could not see anyone. The child, a budding medium, could clearly see spirits and communicate with them. As punishment for using her gift, she was sent to stand in the corner and missed out on treats that the rest of the family received whenever she had conversations with spirits. This child spent a lot of time crying and even though confirmation was given by an outsider about the child's capabilities it was unacceptable proof to the mother that her child had a gift.

Another example of such misunderstandings happened when a young empathic boy visited his cousins one summer. The family's pet hamster was accidentally dropped when one of the cousins mishandled it. The young empath immediately cried out that the hamster's back was broken from the fall. As a result of this outburst, the young empath was misunderstood and ridiculed for expressing the shared pain of the pet

Be observant of your children. For example, if you take your children to a large, busy department store or mall and your child begins to get stomach aches or puts their hands over their ears as if to stop the noise – pay attention. It is possible that your child is empathic and is picking up the overwhelming energy of all the customers in the store. Any large center can have the same effect on these children – stadiums, concerts, fairgrounds, etc. The child can also be affected by a smaller group of people who are in a constant state of strife. The empathic child can become ill from the onslaught of emotions without proper guidance.

The Spiritual Gifts

Another instance of spiritually gifted children was observed in a preschool day care program when the workers noticed a toddler who often stood alone while engaging in conversation with no one who could be observed. The child who was about 18 months old and had not yet mastered his native language was speaking age-lic fluently. Superstitious beliefs of the employees ran wild and the parents were asked to find another school for their toddler.

If you make your child feel bad because they have metaphysical experiences, you are not only invalidating their gifts, you are criticizing their core individualism. If you don't understand what they are experiencing, research it and find helpful information or a spiritually enlightened person who can help your child transition into the full blessing of their gifts.

It is not only the youngest who are having these experiences. Adults, teens and children alike can become open to spiritual gifts from near-death-experiences (NDE) or out-of-body-experiences (OBE). Any brush with the spiritual world changes a person. How could it not when everything you have been taught has just been proven different?

Many of you reading these words were born with spiritual gifts but as young children you used your abilities in a child-like manner with innocence and without guile. As a result perhaps your parents or older siblings ridiculed or shamed you into putting away these capabilities. Keep in mind that being sensitive to the spirit was often labeled or described as being fragile or having a weak constitution. You may have been told by a concerned parent that you were different as their fears tried to shape you into a preconceived mold of what was normal. Children especially have a difficult time holding onto their individuality under such pressures.

Be open to the possibilities and listen without judgment when you or someone you know has experiences that are unfamiliar to you. There is a lot more of the unseen and mysterious Universe than what you can see with your natural eyes.

Chapter 5

Evidence of Spiritual Gifts

Today many of you are experiencing symptoms or indicators that were unfamiliar to you in the past but are quite familiar now in this time of transition. You may have one or two of these signs or you may have many. Even one or two signifies that a change is taking place in your life and that you are being prepared for a transition. Reading the list opens you to the possibilities of allowing more of these changes to take place in your life now.

Use the following list of indicators to gauge the progress of your preparation for what is ahead:

- You awaken at unusual hours during the night.
- You awaken from sleep or a nap aware that your body is vibrating or humming.
- You awaken to discover that an entity is working on you and although it startles you, you do not feel threatened.

- You feel tired during normal hours and feel the need to nap especially when you are unaccustomed to napping.
- You experience an occurrence of napping at the same time each day that lasts for several weeks or months.
- You experience flu-like symptoms – achiness, slight fever, and fatigue -- that disappear within a few days but returns again and again.
- You awaken from sleep or napping feeling as if you have discovered a great mystery.
- You awaken from sleep or napping with solutions that had eluded you before.
- Your doctor can't find anything wrong with you and tells you that your health is better than ever although you feel out of sorts.
- You are dissatisfied with the status quo in your life. You don't enjoy the same things and you question everything you have previously accepted as truth.
- You find yourself lost in thought more often and can become irritable when someone demands your attention.
- You have vivid dreams where you feel as if you have lived an entire lifetime as another person. When you awaken you feel disassociated with your current life.
- You find yourself gazing at the night sky more often as if you are looking for answers.
- You understand that there are no coincidences.
- Your personal life is filled with epiphanies and revelations.

The Spiritual Gifts

- You remember your dreams and desire to discover their meaning or message rather than discount it as only a dream.
- You see the world as bigger than you thought but smaller than you imagined.
- You are getting in touch with your instincts and trusting them more.
- You find that you ask "why" more often than "how".
- You are able to watch with an outside perspective when drama occurs around you, even in your immediate family.
- You have learned not to take life too seriously.
- You read a book that changed your life and everything you had ever believed in or had been taught is now unimportant.
- You experience a letting go of painful memories of the past.
- When you dream you understand it is a dream and you feel as if you are an observer who is watching you dream.
- You experience wisdom and understanding that has previously been considered part of the aging process regardless of your current age.
- You have become more open to learning new ideas and concepts now regardless of your age.
- You no longer feel old or as if you are aging at the normal rate.
- Your ideas about material wealth and possessions have changed from one of more to one of less.

- You realize that nothing is personal. That the things people do have nothing to do with you. They are caught in the web of their own drama or play.
- You look at everyone the same no longer distinguishing anyone by job or title. You see all as members of humankind.
- You notice that you are stronger in every way.
- You have experienced your soul as separate from your body.
- You are sensitive to the unseen world.
- You wake up feeling happy to be alive and grateful for another day in paradise.
- You see other's daily dramas with sadness knowing that they do not have to suffer so.
- You are able to see the truth of a situation when it eludes others.
- Your calm is noticeable to others causing some to want to shatter it if they can.
- Those in your life who are not changing scream insults at you more often but you feel as if you could flick the words away with only a wave of the hand.
- You notice your appetite has changed. Items of food that used to be favorites are no longer of interest. Other foods, that you did not care for in the past, have become desirable.
- You only require five to six hours of sleep each night to feel rested.
- When your gaze falls on another, whether a beggar or the President, you recognize them as another

version of yourself. A different version, true, but of the same essence.
- You are wise enough to understand that you might never know the reason and you can accept that all things have a higher purpose.
- You look forward to sleeping or napping because you know that during this time you are with trusted friends.

Isn't it exciting to see where spirit is taking you!

Chapter 6

Spiritual Gifts for Now and the Future

There are many spiritual gifts. Spiritual gifts are outside the realm of scientific knowledge. A person who possesses spiritual gifts is sensitive to nonphysical or supernatural forces. Another word for the person who possesses these gifts is psychic or someone who perceives beyond the physical and into the spiritual domain.

In this book we will discuss the most common spiritual gifts:

- Empathic
- Creative Force
- Clairsentient
- Clairvoyant
- Intuitive
- Seer
- Reader
- Energy Manipulation

The Spiritual Gifts

- Medium
- Light Bearer
- Kinesiology
- Crossing-Over Departed Spirits
- Healing
- Dream Interpretation
- Faith
- Magnetic Energy
- Sacred Symbols
- Remote Viewing
- Visualization
- Channeling
- Bringing Down the Light
- Bringing Down Energy
- Prayer
- Teaching

The list of gifts presented in this book is not in any particular order and is not listed in a manner that signifies one gift as more important than another. The list is not all-encompassing. There are many abilities and gifts that come from Spirit. Keep in mind that it is possible to have one or more of these gifts working in your life now and that there is no limit to the number of spiritual gifts you can possess.

As you read through the list of The Spiritual Gifts Examined in Part II, keep pen and paper handy to make notes about the gifts that resonate with you. This book is a guide to point you in the right direction and to help you determine your particular abilities. After you have discovered which gift(s) you have, take time to research them in full detail. It is up to you to discover all that you can and to use your gifts to the best of your abilities.

As you read about these spiritual gifts in detail you will be amazed. You may wonder if this is really possible and if some of these gifts are superhuman. It is possible and how else could you describe yourself when you are both physical and spiritual if not superhuman? Our DNA is changing and preparing us for the use of these gifts. These changes will make us stronger, faster and more accurate than ever before.

Isn't it a great time to be alive!

Part II

The Spiritual Gifts Examined

As stated earlier, we will discuss a list of spiritual gifts. As you read and examine each one, try it on for size to see if it feels right for you. The more you understand about these gifts, the more you will understand you own abilities.

Chapter 7

Empathic

To be empathic is to feel the emotions of others. It is a gift that allows you to understand what others are feeling or experiencing. As an empath it can sometimes be overwhelming to be in a large crowd and become inundated by the emotional energy of either so many people or the strong emotions of a few but using you empathic gift to help others is a true blessing once you have mastered the gift.

Signs or indications that you could be empathic include:

- You become easily overwhelmed while in large crowds.
- You feel the intense anger or emotional chaos of others even in small groups.
- You feel claustrophobic or have panic attacks.
- You have stomach problems such as cramping or bowel disturbances in new situations.
- Your ears ring or burn when in crowds or in intense emotional situations.
- You become overwhelmed without apparent reason.

- You seem to absorb the sickness of others and exhibit symptoms similar to theirs that disappear in a few days or weeks.
- You can appear to be a hypochondriac because you feel everything that others feel -- even their illnesses.
- Your doctor cannot find anything wrong with you and your symptoms disappear in a few days or weeks.

Mastering your gift

As with all things whether a gift or a new piece of equipment, you must familiarize yourself with all the aspects in order to use it well or efficiently. Empaths have a unique challenge. Being empathic requires the individual to distinguish their own emotions from the emotional energy surrounding them. Being a successful empath requires the individual to separate their personal feelings from the feelings and emotions that often flood to them from every direction.

It is important to understand your own emotions and feelings so that you can distinguish "you from them". Here are some suggestions that will help you do that:

- Become your own best friend.
- Know yourself from the inside out.
- Analyze your beliefs, concerns and why you feel the way you do about everything that is important to you.

Following these simple suggestions will enable you to know your own emotional energy and to recognize a new or different emotional energy when it comes flooding into your personal comfort zone.

The Spiritual Gifts

Your personal comfort zone is usually an arm's length in diameter. So if you can image or visualize that you are standing in a crowd with you arm pointing straight out in front, then turn in a circle – the diameter formed is your personal zone.

When you pick up the emotional energy of another, they may be several feet or yards away and yet the intensity of their emotional energy can shoot out in any direction and enter your personal zone. This is usually not even an intentional ploy on their part. It just happens. The energy is going in all directions but it does not cause the same reaction in everyone that it encounters; most don't even notice. You notice because you are empathic.

The initial challenge for you is to know yourself so well that you can immediately recognize that the emotion directed toward you is not your own. It feels foreign. You have no understanding of why you would feel that way. The second step is to deflect the energy away. It is not yours and you have no logical reason to accept or own it.

An example of an empathic experience might be something like this: You are in a group of people and someone comes up to introduce himself. You feel an overwhelming and intense romantic interest in this person even though you are in a committed relationship and have never entertained the idea of straying before. It confuses you and you begin to feel guilty and embarrassed.

An empath who is familiar with his/her gifts will immediately catch-on that this is the other person's intense feelings and not her own. An empath who is unfamiliar with his/her gifts can experience internal torture for days or weeks over the encounter because he/she did not understand that the feelings and emotions belonged to the other person.

To master your gift know yourself. Trust what you know about yourself. An empath who has mastered her gift is not influenced by the emotional energy of others. An empath who has mastered his gift is adept at analyzing and compartmentalizing emotional energy.

How this gift is useful

Empaths are capable of perceiving the emotional energy around them and others whether the energy is directed by events, situations or other people. They are able to distinguish where the energy originates and its intent. This gift is a valuable resource during stressful times and disastrous events. The empath is able to assess the mood of the person or event and with wisdom devise an agreeable or amenable solution.

As an example, an empath happens upon an accident where several automobiles are involved. The road is blocked and there isn't any way to get through the scene. While sitting in his car, the empath begins to pick up the overwhelming anxiety of a child crying for his mother. No one can soothe the child because he is too young to express his feelings, he can only cry in anguish which is unsettling to the other accident victims. The empath knows what the child is feeling and can soothe the situation by giving reassurances and comfort to the child which benefits everyone concerned.

The Spiritual Gifts

Tools that help

Empaths require a specific tool that protects them from unnecessary psychic and empathic chatter. They need to protect their personal zone. Here are some suggestions:

1. Visualize a thick membrane shaped like a ball or balloon that encircles your personal zone when you are alone or in a crowd. You can give the ball a specific color if you desire. Visualize that the thoughts and feelings of others bounce off the ball away from you when you are in crowds. While you are safely inside the ball you are able to know your personal feelings only. Spend time inside the ball to examine your personal emotions. If something feels unfamiliar, learn to recognize whether or not it is yours. Practice this so that you can always know your own emotions from those of others. Visualize the ball around you as often as needed. Use it before you become overwhelmed by the emotional energy of others.
2. Visualize an umbrella that completely covers your personal zone when you are alone or in a crowd. You can give the umbrella a specific color if you choose. Any thoughts or feelings of others appear like rain drops only on top of the umbrella – splattering and disappearing without the ability to penetrate your personal zone. Learn to distinguish your own thoughts so that you are aware when the thoughts or feeling belong to another. Practice this exercise often and use the umbrella as often as you like. Use it before you become overwhelmed by the emotional energy of others.

Your Notes:

Chapter 8

Creative Force

Creative force is the ability to create with your thoughts. Everyone has this ability however when it is a spiritual gift it allows you to visualize a situation or scenario with strength and power so that it is easily manifested by the Universe. A person with this gift can easily use their thoughts to change the physical aspects around them by dreaming or visualizing something new.

Signs that you could have the gift of Creative Force:

- Instant manifestation of creative visualization.
- Receiving manifestation of a dream or desire before you have decided it is what you truly want.
- Becoming overwhelmed by the many dreams/choices that manifest.
- You have become afraid of your own thoughts because you have evidence they manifest instantly.

Mastering your gift

It takes practice and persistence to master creative force and without living in the heart it is impossible. From the heart you will create your desires to the highest good of yourself and all concerned. From the heart the creative force is channeled into acts of love for the benefit of all.

Creative force is creative visualization in action. To master your gift you will begin by visualizing small dreams one at a time. You do not move on to the next dream until the current one has become manifest in your life. With each dream you will know the specifics that you desire before you visualize it. If you desire a new job, before visualizing it, be specific by first evaluating your skills and qualifications on paper. Know what job truly suits your characteristics and personality Examine what you don't like about your current job and what you would like in a new job. Carefully examine what you truly want because the results might overwhelm you.

As an example, there was a young creative force who wanted to change careers after being in the same line of work for 12 years. When asked what he did not like about his current work he admitted that it was the same-old repetitive stuff without any true responsibility for the end results; he wanted to be in charge. Either that or it was time to change his career.

Within a week, he was fired from his current job and had three offers to work for other companies. One position was as a one-man show where he would be doing all the work he had done before plus managing an operation even though he had no managing skills or training. Another offer was as a night manager in his same line of work. And the final offer was a completely new career where he would start at the bottom but had the potential for fast advancement.

His creative force had gone wild!

The young man did not know what he truly desired. He had not taken time to evaluate his qualifications and needs which shape a desire into the highest good for all concerned. When these offers came to him, he panicked and actually became ill from wrestling with the pros and cons of each offer and what to do about them.

As a creative force you must know the pros and cons before you start the engine running! You must know what you truly desire by evaluating qualifications plus needs. You must be careful to only manifest the desires of your heart to the highest good of all concerned.

How this gift is useful

The gift of creative force is effective in "moving mountains" so to speak. The individual with this gift can use the creative force of his/her thoughts to direct objects or people out of harm's way or into a different direction often saving lives and thwarting the result of natural or unnatural disasters. The individual with this gift can visualize a different outcome before disaster strikes. The person with this gift can use his/her active imagination to change the course of an event by dreaming a new ending.

Tools that help

Some tools that you might find helpful in becoming adept at creative force;

- Work with visualization techniques. Practice visualizing every day. Learn what works for you and what doesn't.
- Keep a notebook of pros and cons for each desire. Before you create the desire or dream, make sure it is something you truly want.
- Test from the heart for your highest good in the desires you intend to create.
- To create, we must first dream, then visualize, and finally speak the words.
- The Universe/God manifests the desire.
- Faith is a primary force in all things but especially in creative force. Know the level of your faith.

<u>Your Notes</u>:

Your Notes:

Your Notes:

Chapter 9

Clairsentient

Clairsentient is the ability to sense information from objects, locations, persons or events without using any physical methods. A person with this gift can assess a situation about the past or present by allowing their senses to open to the stream of energy that radiates information or consciousness about all things.

Signs that you could be clairsentient:

- You touch a picture or other object and become overwhelmed with images and impressions similar to a movie clip.
- You are in a group of close associates or family members and when you shake someone's hand you are inundated by images of something very violent or unusual that happened to this person.
- You wear gloves because you get icky feelings whenever you touch something or someone.

- Being in close contact with others makes you feel nauseated.
- You know things without being told and the information makes you uncomfortable.
- You say things to people that make them uncomfortable because they know there isn't any way you could have known.
- Others misunderstand your comments and remarks and you don't know where the information came from.

Mastering your gift

To master the gift of clairsentient, like the empath, you must know where the information originates. Is it in you or outside of you? It is important to know your own thoughts and feelings, your own senses and perceptions as well as your vibration.

As with all gifts you must become familiar with all the aspects and how to use them. Using the gift of clairsentience without fully understanding it causes unnecessary grief for you and others.

Start small and work your way up to bigger things. Experiment with your gift. For example, while you are alone prepare to work with the gift of clairsentience. Keep a journal or notebook of each experiment by first make observations about yourself.

Ask and answer such questions as: How do I feel right now? Is anything bothering me? Am I comfortable today? Be sure that you know your own feelings before moving on to the next step.

The Spiritual Gifts

Start with something small and obscure such as a coin or a rock. Place the item in your hand and allow yourself to receive impressions. Notate these impressions in your journal. Ask and answer such questions as: How do I feel now with the object in my hand? Is anything bothering me now that I am holding this object? Is my comfort level the same as it was before I picked up the object? What impressions am I receiving from this object? Practice often.

Next, when you feel comfortable doing so, move on to examine other objects. You might select an item such as a picture or a piece of jewelry that belonged to a relative. Continue with your questions and observations. Notate all information you receive in your journal. Work with the same item for several days before changing to a new item.

Remember to start small and move on to larger things. Always know what you are feeling before you start an experiment with an object or person. Keep your observations in a journal and do not share them with others who might misunderstand.

Learn to control outbursts about the objects with which you come into contact. Learn to censure the information as either appropriate or inappropriate in certain situations. It is not important for you to share every detail of the information you receive. And you must only share when you are directly asked. It is never appropriate to force your clairsentient ability on others. It is however perfectly alright for you to document the impressions you receive in a private journal. It is important that you honor your gift but not at the expense of others. Do not take it upon yourself to push these impressions on others who have not asked for your insights. Be cautious when you are asked to use your gift. Permission to use your gift is not permission to knock someone off their feet with the onslaught of information you have personally received. Be discreet.

How this gift is useful

A clairsentience individual can sense information through contact with objects, places or people. These individuals are capable of receiving short bursts or reams of data through the sense of touch. Those with this gift can use the clairsentience ability to protect and serve the greater good, to help local police or authorities and to help unveil mysteries that cause trauma to others.

An example of using your clairsentient gift might be to help authorities find a missing person. You might touch an article of clothing or a picture of the person and receive information that would help locate them. Or perhaps someone died but the body was never found. Your revelations from a personal item might give peace to a family in mourning.

Your gift is useful in finding people or objects; in giving history or past events regarding places or objects; and unveiling mysteries that surround people, places and objects.

Currently this gift is scoffed at by most police and authorities when it should be embraced.

Tools that help

The most important tool that will help the clairsentient individual is practice. Know yourself and know your gift. Know what you are capable of and what is acceptable to you. Work with the information in the previous section on mastering your gifts. Practice, practice and more practice is the path to successfully using your gift.

Know your preferences. Some clairsentients refuse to work with anything that has to do with death. This is your choice, your free-will. You can choose how to use your gift. You can use it to help others find peace in other ways than finding missing persons. You can help to find missing objects or find the history behind an object. You can use your gift to reveal important facts about the object or person.

Trust the Universe to lead you into the full aspects of your gift and be open to finding the path where your gift is most useful. Always use your gift from the heart.

Your Notes:

Your Notes:

Chapter 10

Clairvoyant

To be clairvoyant means to have clear vision. It is a gift that allows you to clearly see the future and past events of a person, place or object. A person with this gift is sometimes called a seer because they see.

Signs that you might be clairvoyant:

- You feel inundated or overwhelmed by too much information whenever you are away from your regular surroundings.
- You are flooded with images but you don't know what to do with all the information.
- You feel as if your head will burst from the extra perceptions you get in old places such as museums and antique stores.
- You see or know things about others that make you feel uncomfortable.

Mastering your gift

To master the gift of clairvoyance, like the empath and the clairsentient, you must know where the gift originates. It is all too easy to confuse your personal emotions with those of the people around you such as family, friends or co-workers.

Know yourself first so that you can distinguish your emotional energy from the energy you perceive from others. Set up guidelines on how you will receive information – will it come to you through touch or by smell? Will you get mental pictures in the form of snapshots or a movie reel? Know what you can handle so that you can organize the information you receive in a way that is best for all concerned. It doesn't do anyone any good for you to become overwhelmed and burst into tears.

Work with your gift in private and keep a journal to help you fully understand how your clairvoyance is growing and maturing. Keep records of how you are affected by particular places. Are you comfortable in older homes or do you feel the presence of everyone who has ever lived and died there?

Learn to come from heart consciousness whenever you use your gift. Heart consciousness is all the derivatives of love – peace, joy, faith, trust, goodness, joy and the like. If you feel any aspects of fear – anger, control, lack, hatred and similar emotions, stop until you can again come from a place in the heart.

Keep in mind that too much information is too much information. Not everything you see clearly should be shared. Use restraint and discretion when asked for a reading once you have established yourself as clairvoyant.

The Spiritual Gifts

How this gift is useful

The gift of clairvoyance is the ability to clearly see visions or images of the past, present or future. Usually, this gift allows for short moving pictures or scenes to be observed so that the individual is able to know the entire story when working with others. This is a useful tool for healers so that they can understand the root beginning of the disease or illness.

For example, as an energy healer working to release blocked energy it helps to know the original cause. The client you are helping is Asian and speaks very little English. As you lay your hands on the client you are flooded with images of this person when they were a young child working in a factory. You can feel the frustration and pain this person endured. Now you have the root beginning of the trapped emotion and can release it even though the client could not tell you.

Tools that help

The most important tool that will help the clairvoyant is to practice the use of your gift in private before you share it with others. First know yourself and your limitations. Find your comfort zone when working with others. Do not allow others to push you beyond that comfort zone or demand more than you have agreed to give.

A clairvoyant might also find it helpful to use the visualization technique of the ball or balloon encircling them when they do not wish to be disturbed by the visions or images they so easily receive – see Empathic.

It is ok to have office hours or hours where you are not on duty. Use the ball to protect your personal zone when you don't want to work or be inundated by your gift.

Your Notes:

Your Notes:

Your Notes:

Chapter 11

Intuitive

An intuitive has the ability to know instinctively. The intuitive knows without any explanation, and often without having to think or learn about what they already know.

Signs you might be Intuitive:

- You often say "I know" after someone tells you something.
- When you are in a new situation, it doesn't feel new to you.
- You walk into a room and no one has to explain what happened five or ten minutes before, you already know.
- You watch others work in a field where you have no experience but you are able to understand what needs to be done to complete the project and even make suggestions.

- You find yourself getting angry or impatient when someone gives instructions to you because you already know what they are going to say.
- No one can throw a surprise party for you or make plans without your knowing.
- When two people are arguing, you know the solution that would solve their problem.
- You know when the phone will ring before it rings.
- You know who is on the phone before you answer it.

Mastering your gift

Like so many of the other gifts – empath, clairsentient, clairvoyance, and others – being an intuitive is being sensitive to the emotional energy around you. You are picking up the emotional energy and intuiting or discerning its implications and meaning.

To master your gift you must learn to use discretion and wisdom when reading the emotional energy or atmosphere around you. Not everyone appreciates your knowledge of their particular situation so it is important that you learn to use the heart as a barometer in all intuitive situations.

Allow your heart to indicate the mood or atmosphere around you. The heart will eliminate prideful arrogance at always knowing when others can only guess. Remember that being an intuitive is a spiritual gift and not a weapon.

First work with your gift privately. Practice using your intuitive abilities when you are alone. Begin by asking the following questions: What is the energy in this room? What is the purpose of my picking up this energy? Is there something that I can do to benefit another by knowing this? If there is, what can I do to benefit someone else? If not, what do I do with the information? Am I picking up energy that is distracting from the main energy? Write the questions and their answers or impressions in a private journal. Work alone until you feel confident that you can take the experiment into a small setting or group of people. Mentally ask the same questions you asked before when alone, then remove yourself from the group and notate your journal of both the questions and the answers.

In practicing these techniques you are allowing yourself as well as your gift to grow and mature. You are learning to be discreet and confidential. You are learning to weed out the distracting energy that would keep you from the true purpose of your gift. These are traits that are desirable in a gifted intuitive.

How this gift is useful

An intuitive knows what others cannot know without study and reflection. A person with this gift has the ability to quickly get to the gist of a matter. This gift is beneficial in mediation between parties that cannot come to an agreement on a matter of intense dispute. It is also beneficial in interrogation and in negotiation processes between individuals, companies or countries. Your gift is of great value when you have mastered it otherwise you are seen by others as just another know-it-all.

Tools that help

The most important tool that will help an intuitive besides discretion and humility is to develop an ability to decipher the unimportant energy patterns from those that have the true message. In order to do that you can visualize that the energy is coming toward you in colorful streamers. The important message is red in color while the unimportant messages are yellow or green or shades of blue. Visualize that you grab the red streamer and flick the other colors away from you so that they simply flutter around the room without distracting you. Practice this alone and then again in a small group before you begin to depend on it in larger more intense situations.

Your Notes:

Your Notes:

Your Notes:

Chapter 12

Seer

A seer is one who sees (also see clairvoyant) through a combination of methods. The seeing might be triggered from touching an object or by a thought of a person, place or thing.

Signs you might be a Seer:

- You find that you often say "I see" when someone is talking to you or telling a story.
- You see an actual picture when someone is reading aloud or telling a story.
- You cringe when someone makes a remark about something embarrassing or painful because you see it as clearly as if you were present when it happened.
- You have been told you have a vivid imagination.
- You can read between the lines in almost every situation.

- You see problems or possible collisions before they happen and are usually able to avoid them.
- You role play before important meetings so that you can "see" how the event will play out.
- You receive visions that fill in the blanks when others are talking about personal situations.

Mastering your gift

Like the empath, clairsentience, clairvoyant and intuitive, your gift is tied to the sensations you receive from the emotional energy around you. You use the sense of sight to interpret that energy.

The mastery of your gift requires that you separate the important aspects of what you see from the less important. This takes time and practice.

First, take charge of your gift. You do not have to receive messages or vision 24 hours a day. You can set boundaries on when and where you will use your gift. Stay firm about this but do not become rigid. There will be certain times when you must use your gift outside of normal business hours.

Second, know yourself. You must know your own thoughts, ideas, and daydreams or visual images before you can separate the important from the less important aspects of your gift. To do this, work alone and keep a journal about your discoveries. Begin by asking and answering the following questions: What am I seeing right now? Who does this concern? Is it important? Is there a message in this vision? Is the message for me? Is the message for another? What is the specific message? Write the questions and their answers in your private journal. Practice this exercise alone until you are comfortable before taking the exercise to a small group. Repeat the process in the small group but then excuse yourself and notate all the information in your journal as you did before. Practice this step for a while before using your gift in a larger group.

Remember that you are given sensitive information about others and this requires discretion. Never force your visions on others. Always wait until someone asks you to use your gift before sharing. Make certain that the information you share is only for the person it involves. Never share private information in a group setting. If necessary, tell the person you will share with them in private at a later time.

How this gift is useful

A seer sees what is hidden to others. An individual that has mastered this gift has the ability to see into the heart of the matter with clear focus. They see the circumstances and the intent behind the individual action. It is difficult if not impossible to lie to a seer.

This gift is useful when finding anything hidden. For example you could use your gift to locate stolen property, missing persons, or the underlying meaning of a business venture. You can also shed light on why certain events happened. Sometimes, the bereaved can't let go of their loved one until they understand why their death happened.

With the gift of Seer, you have the ability to give to others and to help them find acceptance and understanding.

Tools that help

As you work with your gift of Seer, the most important challenge is to separate the important aspects of your visions from the less important. In order to do this you will visualize that your brain receives all energy freely and easily. Visualize that inside the brain there is a compartment that has two drains, one that collects the important data and one that allows the unimportant to wash away and return to its source. Visualize that you are only concerned with the important data as it collects in a basin waiting for you to examine it. Visualize that the data flow has stopped for the time being and that you now examine the important data that has collected. Practice this visualization often so that it becomes the natural receiving process for all data you receive.

Your Notes:

The Spiritual Gifts

Your Notes:

Your Notes:

Chapter 13

Reader

A reader has the ability to read other people and situations. They do not read the mind of others as this would be an invasion of free-will but they do read the energy of the person or situation and can predict what will happen based on the current energy.

Signs you might be a Reader:

- You know when someone is getting angry before they do.
- You know when someone is lying to you.
- You know when a couple is having relationship troubles before they admit it.
- You sense the sexual orientation of others.
- You know when someone is trying to hide something from you or others.
- You know when to leave because you sense when the energy is becoming volatile.

- You know when someone has a hidden agenda even if you haven't yet figured it out.
- You trust your immediate impression of others whether good or bad.
- You know and understand body language.
- You know the leader in any group even when they try to hide it.
- You sense when something is wrong or off in almost any situation.

Mastering your gift

To master the gift of Reader requires practice and an innate ability to understand action and reaction. The most important skill you can practice as a reader is to first know yourself and your own actions and reactions.

Spend private time examining your own actions and how others react to you. For example, make notes on the following: When I do ____, others do ____. Make journal entries about ever action you take and the reaction of others. Notate your experiences in detail. After you are completely comfortable with that, move forward by using the same technique to examine the actions and reactions that others have. Keep good notes on what you discover.

As a reader you are already using energy patterns as a guide. To become a gifted reader you will need to understand the Spiritual Law of Cause and Effect, or action and reaction. So do not be afraid to add knowledge to your understanding. This only strengthens your gift.

The Spiritual Gifts

How this gift is useful

A reader has the ability to read the current mood or emotional energy of a situation or person. With this gift, the reader can predict the next chain of events.

The gift of Reader is useful in personal and business transactions. As a reader you are able to discern the underlying reasons that people make the decisions they do and predict with accuracy how an event will play out.

Tools that help

As a reader you must master the ability to know what is important and what is not important in a given situation. The underlying reasons that affect the decision people make is not the same for everyone. As you read a situation, you must learn to discern what the priority is and discard what is not. It is a delicate balancing act.

The most useful tool is to return often to the directions in mastering your gift. Practice these steps again and again.

Your Notes:

Your Notes:

Chapter 14

Energy Manipulation

A person with the gift of energy manipulation can effectively deflect or redirect the energy of a person or event. This is especially useful in volatile situations for the energy manipulator can protect the innocent by directing protective energy fields around others or by deflecting negative energy away from others.

Signs that you might be an Energy Manipulator:

- You have miraculously avoided an accident.
- You have seen a potential disaster averted.
- You screamed stop at an event and it stopped.
- You visualized how an event would occur and it happened exactly as you planned.
- You have the ability to change your dreams.
- You observe your dreams as you are dreaming.
- You understand that life is only a dream.
- You are aware of the energy surrounding your body.

- You gather energy into a ball and play with it, tossing it back and forth between your hands.
- You are aware of the energy of others.
- You have been moved backward or forward by unseen energy.
- You have felt a great force of energy descend on you from above causing you to become weak in the knees or have to sit down.
- When in meditation you have felt energy enter through you crown chakra and you instinctively feel the need to release the energy through the root chakra into Mother Earth.
- You find it easy to work with the energy of your chakras and can clearly see the colors of each.
- You are influenced by the Earth's magnetic fields and meridians.

Mastering your gift

To master the gift of energy manipulation requires harnessing what you already know. You are aware of energy and that it has a tangible effect on you and others.

If you have not yet followed the directions in Step One, do it now. Let the heart always be your guide on when and how to use or manipulate energy. Move into the heart before you practice any of these suggestions.

You will find it helpful to work with energy in small steps before moving on to more complicated tasks. First, practice feeling the energy by placing your hands over each other but without touching. You will feel the energy between the palms of your two hands. By moving your hands further away, you will feel the energy stretching and by moving your hands closer you will feel the energy tighten into a smaller but stronger ball or force. Practice this small exercise often to strengthen your concept of energy.

Later, you might add inflated balloons to the practice. Put the balloons on a flat surface, one or two is sufficient, and wait for the energy between your hands to be at its strongest. Next roll the energy between your hands and throw it at the balloons. Practice until you can move the balloons across the flat surface. Keep in mind that you are successful when the energy moves the balloons, not the wind or force of the throw. Focus your attention so that the energy shoots out of your hands toward the balloons.

Mastering this small step opens the gift of energy manipulation to other possibilities. Practice, practice, practice, but always from the heart.

How this gift is useful

The gift of energy manipulation is the ability to direct energy patterns and focus from one location to another. Many can use this gift to send energy where it is needed most, currently into Mother Earth and to a specific location on the planet such as the oceans or seas. This is a great healing and restorative tool because blocked energy causes disease and illness in every energetic being.

As an Energy Manipulator, you can send healing energy or the energy of love to areas that have gone through natural disasters such as hurricanes, earthquakes, tsunamis or tornados. It is also within your power to divert the energy of natural disasters to less populated locations thereby saving the loss of many lives and properties.

Tools that help

The tools most beneficial to the energy manipulator are to practice working with energy as often as possible but always from the heart. When you live in the heart you will know instinctively how and where to use your gift. The heart will guide you. And it is from the heart that the gift is strengthened. Otherwise, you only have the signs of being an energy manipulator without the force of love behind it.

Your Notes:

Your Notes:

Your Notes:

Chapter 15

Medium

A medium has the ability to see and communicate with incarnated or disincarnated souls. This gift is especially useful when the dead have unfinished business or when the soul has a message for the body.

Signs that you might be a medium:

- You still see spirits after the age that others have stopped seeing them.
- The spirits you see appear to be as real and tangible as your friends and family.
- You hear the spirits communicating.
- Spirits seem to be attracted to you because you see them everywhere you go.
- The spirits seem to want you to do something for them but you are reluctant and wish they would go away.

- You have been medicated and diagnosed with a mental disorder because of this ability, maybe as early as your teens.
- Few believe you when you relay messages from spirits.
- You self-medicate with drugs or alcohol because this is the only way you have found to drown out your ability to see and hear spirits.
- You think you must be crazy since you are the only one you know who has this ability.
- You do not think of your gift as ability or blessing but rather as a disability or curse.
- You have given up on being normal and think of ending your life.
- You feel that the unseen world is torturing you by these visitations.
- You have been told by others that you are possessed or cursed by God.
- You are afraid of the spirits and you try to hide from them without success.
- You have become an outcast among family and friends.

Mastering your gift

To master the gift of Medium, you must first accept that you are different and unique with a unique ability. You have a capability that others do not have. This is something to be treasured. You also must come to the realization that others are locked into a system of belief that has been handed down for centuries and is based in fear. By accepting your gift and

The Spiritual Gifts

using it to its fullest degree, you can perhaps shed light into their narrow way of thinking and open a doorway to a new freedom.

First, live in the heart and learn to recognize love. Love and fear cannot occupy the same space. It is in love, from the heart, that you will find liberty. When you live in the heart, you lose the fear of departed or disincarnate spirits and replace it with love. Love accepts all things as they are, neither good nor bad, simply what they are. Spirits in themselves are not either good or bad. It is your belief system about them that categorizes and labels them by such degrees.

Accept that you have a unique gift, that you have the ability to do this or you would not have been given it and get started. Choose love and it will soon seem as easy as sliced pie.

How this gift is useful

A medium has the ability to see and talk to departed spirits and disincarnate beings. A medium uses their gift to give others messages from the dead. This gift is often used to assist a departed soul so that it can return to the light. Often these souls feel as if they cannot leave until their message is heard or delivered to the living. A medium uses their gift for this purpose.

Tools that help

Work with your gift in private before going into a larger group. You can easily accomplish this by organizing how you will receive or talk with spirits. Utilize your spiritual companions or spirit guides. They are here to assist you but you must take the first step by asking for their assistance.

First, set up some boundaries. For example, ask you spiritual guides to allow only those with simple messages to come through to you between 2:00 PM and 4:00 PM. This is only an example but it allows you see that you can set up limits. Another boundary you can establish is that your guides set up a protective barrier around you from all spiritual contact that is not an emergency between 6:00 PM to 6:00 AM so that you can have a normal social life.

The possibilities are endless when you realize this gift is a blessing that you can work with on your own schedule and terms rather than a curse of being tortured day and night by these anxious souls. Make notations in a journal of how you want to use and operate this gift. Start small. If you find later that you want to make changes and that you are capable of expanding your hours or doing more with your gift, you can always change it. Be sure to notate the boundaries and limitations in your personal journal.

The second tool that will help you to master your gift is to set up a list of rules that will be followed. For example, there are certain things that you will do and other things you will not do. You need to be clear about this in your own mind first, and then notate it in your journal. Next you will relay the rules to your spiritual companions and finally relay the rules to the departed spirits who come to you. An example of a rule you might incorporate is that you are not willing to travel over 20 miles to help the spirit with unfinished business. That if the task is further than 20 miles away that you will write a letter. Again, this is only an example but you want to

The Spiritual Gifts

incorporate something similar in your rules. Remember that you set the boundaries, the limits and the rules of your gift.

Always center yourself in the heart and you will find the answers you seek in order to use your gift to the best of your ability and to the highest good of all concerned.

Your Notes:

Your Notes:

Chapter 16

Light Bearer

The light bearer brings the light to all and shines the light in dark places. A light bearer's presence shines the light which is similar to a spot light without discrimination or intent. The light is simply a part of the individual and will shine where it will. The individual who has this gift appears radiant to others but can also makes others uncomfortable because the light bearer's spotlight reveals their flaws or dark places.

Signs that you might be a Light Bearer:

- Others are uncomfortable around you.
- You have been told that you are too perfect.
- You have been told that you are a mirror reflecting back other's imperfections.
- You are equally comfortable alone or in a crowd although you prefer to be alone.
- Individuals eventually show their ugliest side to you.

- Others try to convince you to drink or try a drug in hopes it will dim your light.
- People open up to you in an attempt to elicit your understanding of their excuses.
- People think you know everything about them and feel scared, shy or uncertain around you.
- Some gaze at you with starry and worshipful eyes.

Mastering your gift

Mastering the gift of light bearer comes from the understanding that the light you bring to dark places has nothing to do with you. It is a gift of God that is always showing everyone the way home, the pathway to their highest good. The reaction that others have to the light you bear has nothing to do with you. You simply carry the light and you are often unaware of the light and what it reveals. Each person who comes into contact with the light has a different reaction to it but you must keep in mind that it is not your light they are reacting to. It is the Light of God that you bear wherever you go.

The light is attached to you much like a permanent lantern in your hand. You cannot set it down or discard it. It is a part of who you are and your Divine gift.

To master your gift practice being totally conscious of the light that accompanies you everywhere you go. Practice acceptance of this gift that is a total and complete part of you. Before, you were confused about the reaction of others but now you know that their reaction has nothing to do with you. Visualize that you meet someone new and their reaction is to shy away from you. In the past this felt hurtful, but now that you know the truth you can accept that their reaction is to the light you bear and not a personal affront to you. Next visualize how you will react to them. You will smile and accept your gift with gratitude knowing that you are whole and complete. You will utter gratitude or a prayer of thanksgiving that you were able to bear the light to that person in need.

In general, to master your light bearer gift, your attitude shifts from one of worry and misunderstanding to one of gratitude and understanding. This is the key to mastering this gift.

How this gift is useful

The light bearer brings light to dark places whether the dark place is a personal situation or a group event. The light bearer does not control the light; he/she simply carries the light. The light does the rest.

The light reveals what can be changed to the highest good of all concerned in the individual or group. That is all that it does. It does not condemn or judge. The light merely clears a path of greater understanding.

For example, as a light bearer you pass through a group of people whose foremost desire is to experience pleasure. You don't know this; you are merely passing through a crowd. The light you bear shines on their desire and they clearly see the wasted years of pursuing only pleasure. You move on through the crowd into another group of people whose foremost desire is personal gain regardless of the cost. As you pass through this group, the light you bear shines on this desire and they have a moment of clarity on the price they have paid for their desire.

Each of these groups now has an opportunity for change and that was the purpose of the light. It shines in dark places and gives hope for change. You bear the light to all with whom you come in contact.

Tools that help

The most important tool for the light bearer is acceptance. Practice acceptance now. Do not take your gift as personal rejection. Accept that you have a gift that can sometimes create discomfort but for most it brings hope of change and reconciliation.

To practice acceptance is to understand God's love and that all things have their purpose. There is a purpose for light and also for darkness. It is a higher purpose, not a personal one. Start by being heart conscious. Follow the directions in Step One and in this you will find acceptance and peace.

Your Notes:

Your Notes:

Your Notes:

Chapter 17

Applied Kinesiology

Applied Kinesiology or muscle testing is not only a gift; it is a tool that is beneficial to all that use it. A person who has the gift of kinesiology uses it to find truth in all matters.

Signs you might have the gift of Applied Kinesiology:

- You find that you test the truth of everything.
- You are amazed at the accuracy of muscle testing.
- You study all that you can about this tool.
- You refuse to accept the criticism of others about using applied kinesiology.
- You use several different techniques of applied kinesiology. One to use in private, and others to use when you are around other people or in a crowd.
- You use applied kinesiology to talk to your spiritual companions or guides.

- You encourage others to master the techniques even teaching it to others or writing articles about it.
- Using muscle testing has become second nature to you.

Mastering your gift

To master the gift of applied kinesiology or muscle testing requires lots and lots of practice. As with all the gifts, the more you know the better. To begin, become familiar with the different techniques used and find the one that works best for you. Some use the arm out to the side, others use the index finger and thumb, while still others us the entire body. All of these techniques are excellent. Pick one and work with it on a daily basis in private. There are excellent resources on the web that give diagrams and YouTube has videos that you can watch to educate yourself on techniques. After you have learned a technique, use the following instructions for practice.

First, center in the heart and make a series of statements that you know to be true and test their accuracy or truth. For example, if you are female you will make the statement: I am female and then test the truth of the statement. Make other statements such as: My name is ____. I am ___ years old. I drive a _____ automobile. Work with this for several days before moving on.

Next make a series of statements that you know to be false and test their accuracy. For example, if you are female you will make the statement: I am male and then test the truth of the statement. Make other false statements such as: My name is ____. I am ____ years old. I drive a ____ automobile. Work with this exercise for several days before moving on.

Finally you will make a series of statements that you do not know whether they are true or false and test for their accuracy. For example, make the statement: The next phone call I get will be from ____. Then test the truth of the statement. Keep records of your accuracy. Think of other statements you do not know and test the truth of those too. Make sure this set of statements are ones that you do not know but that you can find out later whether or not they are true or false.

You will have mastered this gift when you fully understand that your body cannot lie to you and that you can use this gift to help others and yourself to the highest good of all concerned.

How this gift is useful

The gift of applied kinesiology is testing for truth from the heart. Many use applied kinesiology but fail to involve the heart in the testing process. When the heart is not involved you can receive false-positive answers. Applied Kinesiology is not a lie detector test and should not be used in this manner. The gift of applied kinesiology consistently test the truth of a matter for the highest good of all concerned.

Those who get the most from this gift are concerned about the good of all. Muscle testing is an effective tool when desiring to get to the truth of a matter. It brings understanding and faith when used appropriately.

Tools that help

There are many visualization techniques for those working with the gift of applied kinesiology. First and foremost, you will center yourself in the heart before using any testing techniques. The following exercise is helpful:

- Visualize that you are sitting in lotus position in a protected space. Now place your hand over your heart organ and listen to the heartbeat. Follow the heartbeat with your breath. Center yourself in the heart. Work with this until all the instructions flow naturally and flawlessly and you feel one with the heart.

Your Notes:

The Spiritual Gifts

Your Notes:

Your Notes:

Chapter 18

Crossing-Over Departed Spirits

Crossing-over departed spirits is the ability to help spirits find their way home. A person with this gift can sense the spirits are near and what they want. A person with this gift is not necessarily a medium because they do not always see the spirits or hear them. A person with this gift also has the ability or gift of bringing-down the light so that the departed spirits can cross through a doorway into the light.

Signs that you might have the gift of Crossing-Over Spirits:

- You are conscious of the unseen.
- You know that you are not alone.
- You have worked with white-light and understand its power.
- You work with applied kinesiology and use it to confirm what you already know.
- You are not afraid of disincarnate souls.
- You already work with energy and understand that energy never dies.

- You have a deeper understanding of the afterlife and you are frustrated that there is confusion about what happens after death.
- You have had experiences with flickering lights and electronics and sense that someone is there in another dimension.
- You desire to see the unseen.
- You believe in reincarnation as a fundamental process of life.
- You trust God/Universe to only allow experiences that you can handle.
- You understand that there are different planes of existence and that a soul can become trapped.
- You have the ability to astral travel.
- You can easily get from one plane of existence to another.
- You are fearless.

Mastering your gift

To master the gift of crossing-over departed spirits there are a few steps you must take. First, set aside a time and place to work with this gift. You should pick a time of day when it will be easy to do this work every day. The place should be where you will not easily be disturbed, away from family members and pets is best. If you have already been working with applied kinesiology or muscle testing you can use this to find out when the departed souls are present. Finally, you speak to the departed souls and give information on the process you will use. For example, you will tell them the rules of the procedure such as, "Hello. My name is _____. I am here to help you cross-over to the other side. Please form a line in an orderly fashion facing toward this _____ because this is where the doorway will open. The doorway will stay open until each one has crossed-over so there is no need to feel anxious. When you are at the front of the line, please look into the other side. You will see someone waiting for you. Go to them; they will help you the rest of the way. That makes room for the next one in line and so forth. God bless and Namaste."

This is the basic process that has been used successfully in the past by others who cross-over souls. You can start with it and then when you feel more comfortable vary the process to something more suitable to your personality and taste.

One of the most important concepts is to let this become a daily ritual – same time, same place – each and every day. You will find that word gets around and you will have a growing line of departed souls waiting for you to cross them over each day. Another important concept is that you set boundaries. In the evening, if you do not wish to be awakened by anxious souls ready to cross-over, make a statement before retiring: "As mistress/master of this home, we will all rest undisturbed." With this simple statement, the departed souls must wait for you to get started at your usual time and place.

How this gift is useful

Crossing-over departed souls is useful to both you and the departed soul. You receive a great deal of satisfaction from working with this gift. The souls you cross-over are finally able to transition and return to the Source of All.

Tools that help

The gift of crossing-over departed spirits or souls does not require any specialized accompanying gifts such as clairvoyance or being a medium. It requires only a willingness to do this work. It is however necessary that the individual be intuitive and sensitive to the spiritual realm so that they will sense when spirits are waiting to cross-over.

Tools that help include the ability to visualize, bringing down the white light in order to open the doorway into the other side and the use of muscle testing to check-in with your higher self or spiritual companions. You will want to test for truth that the departed souls are present, following your directions and crossing-over once the doorway has been opened.

Your Notes:

Your Notes:

Your Notes:

Chapter 19

Instinct

The gift of instinct is similar to the gift of intuition in that the person with this gift knows instinctively what action is necessary without having to think about it and they know instinctively when things are about to happen. They trust their instincts or gut feelings.

Signs you might have the gift of Instinct:

- You have frequent stomach aches or headaches.
- You have been diagnosed with irritable bowel syndrome (IBS) or migraines.
- You feel a charge or change in your body before important events actually happen.
- You have been known to have the hair on the back of your neck or arms stand up when others don't sense anything.
- You just know and you trust it.
- You have been in a situation where you felt an urgent need to leave. Later you discovered that by

following the guidance you were spared from a disaster.
- You do a "gut check" before making decisions.
- You often feel the need to sleep on things before making any major decisions.
- Sometimes you get an urge to act first and analyze later.
- You feel protected and led to do certain things.
- Your actions appear rash to others but they haven't failed you.
- You have an uncanny ability to avoid disaster.

Mastering your gift

To master the gift of Instinct is to trust it. As with the other psychic gifts such as intuition, empath, clairaudience and clairvoyance, you need to start small before taking your gift into a larger group.

It helps to first practice and work with your gift in a private place. Keep a journal of your progress. It will be invaluable to you as your abilities grow. Work with personal experiences that are current in your life. For example, perhaps someone in your family is beginning to date or start a new relationship. With this particular situation in mind ask the following questions: What is my instinct telling me about this situation/person? Do I feel this in my gut? If not, where do I feel a physical correlation to this instinct? Is this person or situation trustworthy?

This is only an example of the types of questions you can work with but it gives you a starting point. Be sure to notate all the questions and answers in your private journal. Also notate the actual results when it becomes apparent. For example, were your instincts about this person or situation accurate?

The second most valuable practice is to learn the art of discretion. The master of the gift of instinct never forces information on others and is not intrusive in the affairs of others. You must only use your gift in regard to others when asked. There are plenty of opportunities to utilize your gift besides revealing private information. The private information you gather is to only be used as an instructional tool.

Practice using your gift first on personal matters and then use it on larger, unrelated matters. For example, you might ask what your instincts are telling you about the weather or the economy. Your questions will be similar to the ones asked on personal matters: What are my instincts telling me about the tropical storm off the coast of Florida? Do I feel this in my gut? If not, where do I feel a physical correlation to my instincts about this event? Will this storm cause major damage? Be sure to notate the actual results when it is apparent by asking: Were my instincts about this event accurate?

As with all gifts, you will come from a place in the heart to use this most effectively.

How this gift is useful

The gift of instinct is a deep trust in the ability to be guided and directed by these intuitive feelings that emanate from the heart or fourth dimension even though the effects of the ability are often found in other parts of the body such as the sacral and the third eye chakra. A person with this gift follows the leading of spirit often without knowing why. They simply trust.

Using the gift of instinct often allows you to warn of impending disasters and to help others escape harm. It is not designed to be used as a means to lessen the personal experiences of life or to avoid living. It is meant to serve the greater good.

Tools that help

An exercise that helps you develop your gift of instinct is simply to keep a recorded journal of those instincts. Written documentation is proof that you can rely on your instincts. It goes a long way in boosting courage and faith in your abilities.

Your Notes:

The Spiritual Gifts

Your Notes:

Your Notes:

Chapter 20

Dream Interpreter

The gift of Dream Interpreter is the ability to decipher dreams for yourself and others. This gift completely trusts the heart for the explanation or interpretation of signs and symbols within the dream itself.

Dream interpretation is of great benefit because dreams are sometimes confusing and often forgotten. Dreams are messages from the Universe that help you to navigate through this incarnation.

Signs you might be a Dream Interpreter:

- When you hear others tell about their dream you can see the dream clearly in your mind's eye.
- You recognize the signs and symbols in dreams.
- You have an innate ability to translate the complicated into uncomplicated.
- When you dream, you see yourself as the observer of the dream.
- Others often come to you for understanding.

- You are seen by others as wise.
- Your opinion is respected regardless of your age.
- You have the ability to communicate with adults as easily as people your own age.
- You understand that the life you live is merely a dream that can be changed at any time by your desire.
- You see dreams as messages.
- When you have a problem, you ask for the solution to be revealed during your dreams and it is.
- You find it easy to move between spiritual realms while in meditation or other spiritual pursuits.
- You are contemplative and slow to action or reaction.
- You often see beyond the current situation and into the possibilities.

Mastering your gift

To master the gift of Dream Interpretation you must accept that the actual message comes through from your higher self and through your connection to the All.

For example, a friend reports a dream to you about being in a corridor with many doors on either side. He tried to open each door but none would open. He began to feel panicky because he wanted to find the way. He felt lost because none of the doors would open. He saw others in the corridor and they were able to open doors and go inside but none of the doors he tried would open. He felt distraught and lost as if he would never find the way.

As a dream interpreter you understand that none of the doors in that corridor led to his true path; that the direction was not open to him and/or not to his highest good. This is to be revealed to him through you, the dream interpreter. It is not however your place to tell him whether or not the dream related to a career or relationship choice. He will be able to determine this for himself if you pose well-placed questions, such as: Are there any recent changes in your life? Have you made any new choices recently? Do you feel stuck in any area of your life?

How this gift is useful

The gift of dream interpretation is the ability to decipher dreams, their meaning and symbols within the dream for the benefit of yourself and others. The dream interpreter often follows patterns of the dream that can seem illogical to others and puts it into a current perspective for the dreamer.

There has been documentation of dream interpreters throughout history. Many were called upon to decipher the dreams of rulers and kings in ancient times and the bible list several examples of kingdoms being saved from famine or disaster by the interpretation of dreams. Dream interpretation is useful in all aspects of life.

Tools that help

The most important tool you can develop is trust and acceptance of your gift. Always come from a place of love when deciphering dreams for yourself as well as others. Realize that dreams are positive communications that use signs and symbols to transmit needed information.

These signs and symbols can seem strange and even threatening but that is only because of the stigma often attached to them. Look at the dream from the heart and let the heart be your guide. It is from the heart that you will gain understanding that nothing is really good or bad; it is only what it is.

Become familiar with the meaning of signs and symbols. There are currently many books on the subject of dreams that can enhance your understanding. For example, a vehicle or other method of transportation is often a symbol of change; the larger the vehicle the larger the expected change. Moving water also signifies change. A dream of fighting against the current or tide can signify that you are resisting change. These are only a few examples but with a little research and persistence you will soon find that you instinctively know what a dream symbol means.

Your Notes:

The Spiritual Gifts

Your Notes:

Your Notes:

Chapter 21

Healing

The gift of healing is the ability to make another or a situation whole. A person with this gift allows themselves to be a vessel or conduit for Divine energy to flow into the person or situation in need of healing.

The gift of healing often begins with an earnest desire to be a healer and leads to coursework or instruction on a particular modality of healing. Everyone has the ability to heal others and themselves however the gift of healing is the capability to go beyond the modality that has been learned and into the spiritual aspect of being a vessel through which healing energy passes.

Every healer eventually learns techniques of healing by instruction but the gift of Healing usually begins without warning and from the strong desire to intervene in some way.

Signs you might have the gift of Healing:

- You have healed others.

- You are fascinated by stories of miracles and healings.
- You yearn to make a difference and to be of service to others.
- You have had a NDE or OBE.
- You believe that healing is possible.
- You feel your hands grow warm or hot when you think about healing or miracles.
- When you think of others you get impressions of clouds or dark spots depicting disease or illness within their body.
- You can read palms but you can particularly spot current or future illnesses in the lines.
- When you see that someone is hurt, your first instinct is to put your hands on them in hopes they will feel better.
- Dogs and small children come to you automatically.
- You feel that when you do healing work on others a host of spiritual healers are at your side, working alongside you.
- When you are working on others you receive snapshots or motion pictures that show you the root cause of the disorder.
- You follow your intuition when working on others. If you get a message that sheds light on changes that need to be made you boldly relay the information.
- Many have a deep spiritual experience when you place your hands on them in a healing manner.

The Spiritual Gifts

- You have studied many modalities but eventually came up with your own method of healing.
- You desire to be a healer.

Mastering your gift

To master the gift of Healing you must first come from a place of love and oneness. This is only found in the heart. You can have all the training in the world but if it is only head knowledge, your success will be limited. Learn to come from a place in the heart and your success will be unlimited.

How this gift is useful

The gift of healing is useful to restore health and wholeness, to remove disease and disorders, to balance the energetic fields of the body, and to heal the heart organ itself. Of course there are many others uses but these are primary.

The gift of healing starts with the desire to be of service. Do not let others dampen your desire or thwart you from earnestly pursuing this gift. For example, many years ago a young woman was working in the kitchen when her toddler pushed open the screen door getting his fingers caught between the door jamb and the door. She saw the wood cut into his baby fingers and the blood start to spurt. She screamed, "No!"

She knelt down beside him holding his hand between hers and prayed fervently as she comforted the boy. When she opened his hand, the wound was completely healed. Later she relayed the story to her pastor and told him that she thought she had the gift of healing and asked for guidance to develop the gift. The pastor scoffed at her saying that she was too young and that God would not waste the gift of healing on her.

Needless to say, she was devastated and it was close to 15 years before she actively sought guidance and training for her gift of healing.

Tools that help

Become familiar with different modalities of healing and chose one or two that interest you the most. After you have mastered those you can return to the list of options and chose more.

Trust your instincts. Being a healer is similar to being a salesman in that you cannot sell anything you don't believe in. Believe in the modality that you choose, and then learn all that you can about it. Practice it. Offer it to friends and family for their feedback. Have them fill out a questionnaire that is an honest assessment of their experience.

Don't push your healing on others but do make it available.

Learn how energy works and know what to do with excess energy that is released during your healing session. It is always a good idea to use white-light to cleanse your treatment room after you have worked on someone. And it is always a good idea to instruct the negative or excess energy you have released to return to Mother Earth. Our mother takes waste products and turns it into fertilizer. There isn't any type of energy that She cannot convert into positive attributes.

Your Notes:

Your Notes:

Chapter 22

Faith

The gift of faith is the ability to trust the Universe/God that all is as it should be. A person with the gift of faith believes that the greater good is evident in all things seen and unseen.

Signs you might have the gift of Faith:

- You trust that everything is the way it should be.
- You know that there is a higher purpose to all things.
- You pray and know that your prayers are answered.
- You know you are not alone.
- You desire to have faith.
- You see the balance and order in all situations.
- You understand that there are no coincidences.
- You don't take things too seriously and see the humor in life.
- You desire to be in the Universal flow.

- You have learned not to butt your head against a brick wall to force what you want.
- You don't use manipulation tactics; you just trust.
- When something happens that causes pain, you wait to see what will happen next before you determine whether it was positive or negative.
- You understand that things are just what they are, neither good nor bad.
- You follow the leading of spirit even when others ridicule your faith-based decisions.

Mastering your gift

Mastering the gift of Faith is realized by first living in the heart. It is making every conscious effort to look to the heart for all answers and solutions. Faith is a derivative of love; love is God and God-consciousness.

First practice Step One in Part I of this book. Find the rhythm of the heartbeat and jump into it. Live there. Utter words of gratitude in unison with your heartbeat. Let thanksgiving and praise flow throughout the body as the blood circulates throughout the body. Be at peace there and you will find all the faith you need.

How this gift is useful

The gift of faith is the ability to stand firm and unwavering in the belief that all is exactly as it should be; that the Universe/God has everything in perfect order. It is trust from the heart.

Your gift of faith can help others to trust and it can show the way to living in the heart.

Tools that help

The most important tool for the gift of Faith is to begin right now to live in the heart. Practice Step One until you feel one with the heart. This is the key to this gift.

Your Notes:

Your Notes:

Chapter 23

Magnetic Energy

A person with this gift works with the magnetic energy field of the planet and individuals to remove trapped emotional energy and blockages that cause physical, spiritual and emotional diseases and illnesses.

Signs you might have the gift of Magnetic Energy:

- You are deeply influenced when you are near specific energetic vortices such as Sedona or Stonehenge.
- You are aware of your own bio-rhythm and schedule your life accordingly.
- You have noticed that you seem to have energetic periods followed by lethargic periods but have not looked into it further.
- You have been diagnosed as bi-polar.
- Your friends consider you to be eccentric but endearing.
- You feel spikes in your mood, or mood swings that can go from zero to 10 in a matter of minutes.

- Your romantic partner considers you exciting and mysterious.
- You are fascinated by the moon and its cycles.
- Sometimes you feel like the tides, coming and going and always affected by the lunar cycles.
- You have felt trapped in a tide pool and could not escape until the tide returned and washed you back into the natural flow of the ocean.
- You feel most invigorated when you are in the flow.
- You do not enjoy waiting.
- You enjoy the natural pattern of energetic change or cyclic changes.
- You are very interested in any healing technique that uses magnets to change energy patterns.
- The palm chakra in your left hand feels quickened or as if it is a large magnet.

Mastering your gift

To master the gift of magnetic energy, study the use of magnets and their polarity. For example, the simplest understanding about magnets is that they attract other things to themselves. When working as a magnetic healer, you understand that you are attracting (or drawing out) the imbalanced magnetic energy from the client's energy field and onto the magnet you use to do so.

Practice working with magnets or magnetic energy and document what you observe. With each experiment you will run a magnet closely over the area without actually touching it. Use a journal to document your findings. Make sure you

The Spiritual Gifts

notate whether or not the area healed faster than when using traditional methods. Record the following experiments or any others:

- Use on a cut or insect bite.
- Use on a swollen joint or painful swelling.
- Use on the spine of a friend or partner when they have trouble falling asleep to see if it resets their sleep pattern.
- Use to gently rub over the temple area for a headache.
- Use to gently rub over the big toes for a sinus headache.
- Use to rub over the inside of knees for trust issues.

Open yourself to your gift and let it inspire you.

How this gift is useful

The gift of Magnetic Energy is a great tool to use for healing yourself and others. It releases trapped energies in the auric layers around the body so that the person can heal quickly and efficiently from emotional or physical pain.

Tools that help

The most important tool available to you is the influence you already have from magnetic energy. Trust this and use it. The more familiar you become about magnetic energy, the more you will be able to use it to help yourself and others.

Invest in a large magnet that you will use daily. There are many that claim to be the best or top of the line ranging in price from $2.99 to $129.99 plus shipping and handling. I recommend going to your local hardware store and purchasing a regular kitchen magnet that is approximately 3 inches in diameter and has a black knob on it for around $4.50 plus tax. It is sturdy and will last for years

When you purchase the magnet you choose to work with, remember to keep it reserved for your practice only. It is your tool and not used by other members of the family or to hold pictures on the refrigerator. Keep a spare one for others to try when you are telling them about the benefits of working with magnetic energy.

Your Notes:

Your Notes:

Your Notes:

Chapter 24

Sacred Symbols

A person with this gift perceives sacred symbols and their meaning and purposes from beyond the physical plane. They are able to see the geometric shapes and recreate them to give meaning and hope to others. Sacred symbols are invaluable tools for enlightenment.

Signs you might have the gift of Sacred Symbols:

- You see the Divine pattern in all of life.
- You draw or doodle the same pattern again and again.
- You are fascinated by astronomy.
- You look for geometric patterns in spider webs and other acts of nature.
- You enjoy routine.
- You collect abstract works of art.
- Geometric shapes give you a sense of familiarity that cannot be explained.

- You are equally fascinated by black and white or color designs.
- You have an innate ability to accept that you are eternal, that you have been here before and that you will return again and again.

Mastering your gift

The gift of sacred symbols enhances the meaning and history of life. Each religion and culture has its own sacred symbols that originated from basic geometric design such as the circle, triangle, rectangle and square. Many of these designs are combinations of the basic designs which form more complicated symbols such as the octahedron and the tree of life.

To master the gift of sacred symbols one must open their heart to the All That Is – the possibilities and the probabilities. When examining geometric shapes you see beyond the exactness of mathematics to metaphysical concepts such as numerology, Kabbalah, tarot, I-Ch'ing and astrology, etc.

To master the gift of sacred symbols begin by living in the heart. It is the heart that will open the meaning to you. Your second step is to meditate on each fascinating design. Spend time each day contemplating a design. Allow yourself to absorb and be absorbed by the image before you. Keep a journal of your impressions and the understanding that follows for each design.

The Spiritual Gifts

How this gift is useful

The gift of sacred symbols instills spiritual perspective on all things. It allows you to see the Divine design in all of life from the smallest insect to the vastness of the Universes. It is faith-building and mind-expanding. It allows you to give hope to others who cannot see or understand the purpose of life.

Tools that help

Practice using your gift with the suggestions below:

- Meditation – set aside time each day to be alone and undisturbed. Wear comfortable clothing and be seated either on the floor in lotus position or in a chair where your back is straight and feet flat on the floor. Take a few deep breaths to relax then begin by concentrating on a shape. Choose something simple to start like the circle or triangle. After you have meditated on this shape for several days you will understand the complexities of the design and that there is really nothing simple about it. You can meditate on this symbol for a little as five minutes or as long as you like. As you go about your day, look for the symbol to discover how often you see it. You will be amazed how often it appears and how you previously missed it.
- Examination – pick a symbol that you will work with for the next week. Keep a journal of all the places and times you see the symbol for the entire week. Make notations on whether or not the symbol is imbedded or openly in view. After a week, change to a new symbol and repeat the exercise.

Your Notes:

Chapter 25

Remote Viewing

The gift of remote viewing is the ability to sense events, locations or people through the mind's eye or subconscious that is removed from the viewer either by distance or time.

Signs you might have the gift of Remote Viewing:

- You easily and accurately visualize the appearance of someone that you have never met.
- You easily and accurately visualize a place that you have never been.
- Visualization comes easy to you whether in meditation or preparation for an event.
- You get mental images when someone reads aloud.
- You see in pictures or movie frames when others are talking.
- You have an uncanny ability to see potential.

Mastering your gift

To master the gift of remote viewing requires a great deal of practice and record keeping for verification of your accuracy. There are actual tests on the web where you can examine your abilities of remote viewing but it is up to you whether or not you want the developer of the test to know of your abilities.

To practice your skills of remote viewing requires a trusted friend or relative who will be on the other end to assist with the testing material. For example, your assistant will use a picture of a place and its exact location that is known only to him. You will test your accuracy of remote viewing by describing the place in four or five descriptive phrases. Let's say that he has picked a picture of a red barn with snow on the roof beside a river in Idaho. You prove your accuracy by the following phrases: I see the color red; there is a tractor; running water; cold weather; maybe ice or snow.

Notice that these are impressions you have received. It is a very good start. And its takes lots of practice to develop your gift.

How this gift is useful

Many governments use remote viewers to spy on other countries or governments. However to use this gift to your highest good it could be used instead to help authorities find a missing person or to describe what a criminal looks like. It could be used to help someone find a lost object or assist others in selecting the better place to vacation. There are many uses for this gift and when you live in the heart these opportunities will be open to you.

Tools that help

The tool most useful to the remote viewer is practice.

Set aside time every day to work with your gift. As with the other gifts you will want to begin working with your gift in private before taking it to larger groups. Work with a trusted friend to develop your skill. Use different types of media, such as pictures, maps or 3-D images. If your assistant is up to it, have them travel to different places without your knowledge so that you can experiment with remotely viewing their exact location.

There are lots of opportunities to use and develop this tool. A word of caution, do not use this gift to spy on others. It is an invasion of privacy that goes against the divine directive of free-will. When using this or any gift, always start by being grounded in the heart so that you may use the gift to the highest good of all concerned.

Your Notes:

Your Notes:

Chapter 26

Visualization

A person with the gift of visualization has the ability to see or create in the mind's eye. This gift is extremely useful in creating the dreams and desires of the heart for yourself and others.

Signs you might have the gift of Visualization:

- You see what others say rather than hear it.
- You often hear yourself say, "I see."
- For some, it might be easier for you to create images in your mind than to draw them.
- You have been told you have an active imagination.
- You spend a lot of time thinking about things.
- When worried, you can imagine multiple scenarios.
- You worry a lot because you can see the many different possibilities.
- You require a great deal of alone time and like to work independently.

- Your thoughts are very active.
- It is often difficult for you to quiet the thoughts when it is time for sleep or during meditation.
- You have a lot of internal dialogue.
- You read and follow written instructions easily.
- You love to read because a good book is like a real-life movie to you.
- You often experience the characters in a movie or book.
- You don't understand the difficulties others experience when they attempt to visualize.
- It is easy for you to astral travel or jump in and out of other spiritual realms.
- You are an active dreamer.
- For some, you might be artistic.
- You solve puzzles and word or number games easily.

Mastering your gift

To master the gift of visualization is to create with great detail all aspects of the vision or dream. For example, it is not just a new car that you see in your mind's eye; it is a yellow Porsche convertible with black leather interior and teak panels across the dash. You are driving it with the top down and you feel the wind in your hair. Do you see the difference?

Practice your gift with all things that you desire to create in your life. This is where change begins. You create the dream or vision with a much detail as possible; the Universe manifests those dreams and desires.

The Spiritual Gifts

How this gift is useful

The gift of visualization is useful in creating a better world for all. You may start the practice of visualization to create the dreams you desire but it leads to creating for all of mankind. You use your gift for the bigger picture – peace, health, happiness, plenty, and love.

Tools that help

The most important tool for the gift of visualization is meditation. Meditation gives clear focus on creating and visualizing dreams and desires. From the heart you are led to what is needed most in order to change the world into one of fourth dimension – love.

To meditate: Start by sitting quietly and focusing on the heart organ. Place your right hand over the actual location to keep your intent there. Hear the heartbeat; follow its circulation path through the body. Allow gratitude and thanksgiving to fill the heart organ and to circulate through the body. After you have spent several minutes doing the above exercise, just be still. Wait for any insights or realizations that come to you. Allow your natural visualization ability to create from the heart any images you are given. Then send the created image to circulate through the body. Be open to the images. If the images continue, continue with visualizing them in the heart and allowing them to circulate through the body. Do this practice at least once a day.

Your Notes:

Chapter 27

Channeling

The gift of channeling is the ability to hear the messages of incarnated and disincarnated souls or spirits. The person with this gift has the ability to document the message by writing, typing, speaking or using a recording device.

Signs you might have the gift of Channeling:

- You hear voices.
- You hear things that others do not.
- You see and talk to your spiritual guides or angels.
- Your spiritual guides are very real to you.
- You have repeated things you heard from these voices and shocked or surprised others.
- You drink or use drugs to drown-out the voices.
- You practice or use automatic writing when you have a problem.
- You have been diagnosed with a mental disorder.

- You hear things that you cannot see and it makes you feel crazy.
- You feel as if someone is always watching you.
- You feel tormented.

Mastering your gift

Mastering the gift of channeling will only come to you when you accept that there are other dimensions or realms that are active all around you whether you can see them or not. You are not being tormented, you are being contacted. It is your perception that only sees the one aspect of this contact -- fear. Your perception and the perception of the world you live in can only see in third dimension. But there is far more available to you beyond this dimension if you open your heart to it.

The first step is to move into the heart and live in it. Follow the direction in Step One. In the heart, fear goes away for it cannot live in love. In the heart, you know safety and peace. It is here that you will find your full ability and gift.

How this gift is useful

The gift of channeling is very useful to you and others. With this gift you can receive and relay messages from behind the veil to uplift mankind. You will find words of encouragement and hope for your personal life as well as for others.

Some who have the gift of channeling are concerned that they are working with the dead. They are frightened of death. You must understand that death is an illusion. The spirit never dies. The body dies and passes away, but the spiritual entity or soul that you channel is alive is the fullest sense of the word. Alive with love and light!

This gift can also be used to solve problems. The channel can ask for information about particular problems such as how to locate an object or person. However, keep in mind that the spiritual entity you channel will not be forthcoming about any information that changes life paths or history so asking for the winning lottery numbers and such is not the type of information you can get when channeling.

Tools that help

When working with the gift of channeling, start small. If the thought of channeling is frightening to you even though you know instinctively that it is your gift, begin slowly. Start in the heart by following the directions in Step One. After you feel calm and safe, acknowledge your gift with thanksgiving and choose to use the gift. You may want to practice this step several or many times before you actually start the process of channeling.

Next, decide on a method you will use. Will you listen to the words and write out what you hear in response? Will you use pen and paper? Will you use the keyboard or a typewriter? Will you listen and then record the response into a recording device? There are many options, so decide what you will use to begin your first session as a channel.

If you are familiar with applied kinesiology, then you can ask which method is to your highest good and choose that way. If you are adept at muscle testing, you can test each response for accuracy.

Perhaps you wonder about accuracy, but be assured that you have filters that sift the information and responses you are given. These filters can garble the message or enhance it with your own ideas and past experiences. You must be as clear as possible when channeling. It is not uncommon for the channel to repeat the response to the entity and ask: Is that correct? Did I hear you correctly?

Some channels receive pictures rather than words and the pictures are open to interpretation. Be sure to test for accuracy from the heart. Be sure that you are getting the intended message and transcribing it accurately.

Your Notes:

Your Notes:

Your Notes:

Chapter 28

Bringing Down the Light

A person with this gift has the ability to bring down White Light or Divine Light, usually by visualization. This gift is often used during times of extremely stressful or antagonistic situations as a means to calm others. It is also used during meditation, by healers and those who cross over spirits.

Signs you might have the gift of Bringing Down the Light:

- You sense an energy field around you.
- You are conscious of the unseen.
- You know instinctively that white light is God's light.
- You use white light to cleanse and purify.
- You trust white light with all your being.
- You know that white light is the thread that connects everyone to the All.
- You understand that white light is what is left when the body dies.

- You have experienced the effect of white light descending on you.
- You work with other spiritual gifts such as visualization and healing.
- You sense that souls are around you and want something from you.

Mastering your gift

Mastering the gift of bringing down the light requires the ability to visualize. It does not require the gift of visualization but in order to being down the light you must be able to imagine it. Once you can visualize or image the white light coming down then you can direct it.

To master the gift of bringing down the light requires that you fully understand the light is God's light or Universal light. It is from the source of all light. It is all the attributes of love. It cannot be created or destroyed and it cannot be directed to cause harm. When you bring down the white light, you are not creating something new; you are using something that has been here from the beginning.

To understand all that you can about white light meditate on its power and intent from the heart.

How this gift is useful

The gift of bringing down the light can be used to change a situation from fear to love. For example, you see a crowd of unruly teens in the mall parking lot who are out of control. There doesn't seem to be a security guard available and you worry for the safety of others and the teens. You can use your gift of bringing down the light to visualize a great waterfall of

The Spiritual Gifts

white light showering the group with love and light. This will cause a peacefulness to settle over them and the crowd will break-up and disperse within a few minutes.

The gift of bringing down the white light is used by healers to prepare themselves for a healing session, to heal their clients and also to cleanse and purify their work space. The healer visualizes the white light coming down and directs it to the specific task.

The gift of bringing down the white light is used by those who cross-over departed souls. The individual brings down the white light to open a doorway to the other side through which the souls can cross-over.

Tools that help

The first tool you will need to use is visualization.

To practice visualization: Close your eyes and imagine that you have a beautiful red apple in your left hand. You hold a paring knife in your right hand. The hands work together as you press the knife into the peel of the apple near the stem area. Slowly and gently you begin to peel the apple in a circular motion. Around and around, the knife slices gently and with certainty in a complete circle without ever breaking the peel. The apple peel drops onto the counter top and you set the peeled apple beside it. Now pick up the peel and examine it. You smile because when you hold the peeling by the top piece and raise it off the counter a few inches, it again takes the shape of the apple.

If you are successful with the above exercise, then you can visualize successfully. If you are not successful this time, repeat the exercise until you are. You should master this in only a few days of practice.

Once you have successfully peeled the apple in one complete circle you will practice visualizing white light. To do this just close your eyes and imagine a beam of white light coming down from above and pouring into the crown of your head. You feel the energy of white light as it moves through your body, starting at the crown and moving straight down your spine in the direction of your tail bone. Feel the energy leave through the base of the spine. Practice this exercise several times in a row. Your goal is to both feel the energy and visualize the white light as they work together. You can use this method to cleanse the body, the chakras, the auric layers and the soul.

If you were successful with the above exercise, then you can effectively bring down the light. If you were not successful you might find it helpful to stand under a shower and imagine that the water pouring onto the top of your head is white light. Practice this until you no longer need the shower to imagine white light pouring onto the top of your head or crown.

Again, once you successfully visualize white light you can direct it to others, places or events.

Your Notes:

Your Notes:

Your Notes:

Chapter 29

Bringing Down Energy

A person with this gift has the ability to bring down Universal energy also known as chi, ki, and prana. The purpose of this gift is to refresh or energize others or places by filling the chakras or area with new energy. A person who brings down energy can use this gift to heal Mother Earth by sending the energy of love and light into the core of the planet.

Signs you might have the gift of Bringing Down Energy:

- You are conscious of energy around you.
- You feel the energy of others with whom you come into contact.
- You are aware of degrees of energy.
- You are aware of positive and negative energy.
- You feel nauseated when in contact with certain energies or people.
- You feel inspired and uplifted when in the presence of highly enlightened individuals.

- You feel spiritually drained after contact with some energies or people.
- You understand that people battle over energy the same as countries battle over resources.
- You know how to replenish your energy.
- You trust your instincts or gut feelings.
- You trust your perception of the energy you feel from others.
- You are not easily fooled about people.
- You have been told you are very perceptive or observant.
- You might have been diagnosed with a mental disorder in your youth but outgrew it.
- You are aware of magnetic energy and force fields much sooner than others.

Mastering your gift

To master the gift of bringing down energy, you will use your ability to visualize. If you are familiar with energy patterns already then you have sensed the effect of negative and positive energies in many situations. To help you get stated in the practice of visualization see the previous chapter on bringing down the light and use the same methods described to visualize the apple. Once you are successful in visualizing the apple you can work with brining down energy.

Energy or chi, ki, and prana, is the substance or essence of all things material, emotional and spiritual. Energy cannot be created or destroyed but is present in all things. To begin your work with energy first understand that it is already there, you are simply directing it. Perhaps you will give energy a

The Spiritual Gifts

color so that you can imagine that white, blue or green waves are coming down in a vortex or funnel and directed into the core of Mother Earth. You imagine the white, blue or green funnel pouring into an opening then disappearing as it is sucked into Earth and the opening seals around it. Practice these exercises until you feel confident using them.

How this gift is useful

The gift of brining down energy is an excellent method of brining life or refreshing energy where it is needed. Perhaps it is beneficial in places of drought or particularly destructive natural disasters. Often the energy of Mother Earth is taxed greatly or depleted in these areas and with this gift you can refresh the planet.

Other uses might include giving refreshment to individuals or communities that have gone through major crisis or personal losses in their lives. Maybe you use this gift to give a family member hope after devastation or loss. There are many uses of a refreshing nature when gifted with bringing down the energy. Use your gift from the heart and let the heart be your guide.

Tools that help

Visualization is the primary tool that is needed in bringing down energy. Work with the methods already given in this work or find other sources that will enhance your ability to visualize.

Your Notes:

Chapter 30

Prayer

The gift of prayer is the ability to pray for others more effectively than they can pray for themselves. The gift requires a deep faith that your prayers are heard and the ability to articulate the prayer or need as effectively as possible.

Signs you might have the gift of Prayer:

- You have an innate ability to summarize situations efficiently.
- You have an innate ability to simplify complicated scenarios.
- You have faith.
- You believe that God hears prayers and answers them.
- You say what you mean and mean what you say.
- You do not mince words.
- You have been told that you are a straight-shooter when you communicate.

- You seldom ramble or jump rabbits when relaying information to others.
- You can easily focus your attention on the task that needs completion.
- You meditate with ease.
- It is rare for you to experience monkey mind.
- You have never desired to experience drugs or if you did experiment once or twice you did not enjoy it.

Mastering your gift

To master the gift of prayer, simply begin by praying. Your prayer should be succinct and to the point. It is not beneficial to you or those you pray for to utter repetitive words while praying. For example, it is customary for some to kneel and repeat the same words such as, "Oh God, hear me. Oh God, hear me. Oh God, answer my prayer." It would be more beneficial to simply kneel, stand or sit in faith knowing that God hears your prayer before you begin, so begin. The Lord's Prayer is your best example to follow – acknowledgment, praise, and request.

A typical prayer for your Aunt Suzie who has recently lost her beloved husband might be this: Dear God who is holy and wise. Thank you for hearing my prayer. I ask that you bless Aunt Suzie during her time of need with comfort and love. Let her have peace and understanding. Amen.

Another example of a typical prayer for an area that has been devastated by natural disaster might be: Dear God of wisdom and love. Thank you for hearing my prayer. I ask that

The Spiritual Gifts

you bless this suffering community with comfort, love and the faith and energy to rebuild. Amen.

Keep it simple. To do this, think of your own personal life experiences. Perhaps you are a mother or father with a family to raise and a job or other means of support that requires your attention. One of your children needs something from you but when they come to ask they stammer and struggle with the topic. Perhaps they repeat your name again and again or tug at your shirt sleeve or pants leg. Would it not be simpler and more productive if they asked you without hedging or faltering? Wouldn't a direct approach be more appreciated and less time consuming for all concerned? Are you more likely to grant their request due to their persistence or due to their utter simplicity in asking? Use your answers to choose the manner in which you will approach your father or mother.

How this gift is useful

The gift of prayer enables you to be of service to others. With this gift you are capable of praying for individuals, communities, and the world. It is as if you are a great orator on the behalf of the world but without formal, extraneous and flowery presentation. You have the ability to ask for others what they do not know how to ask themselves. Be generous with the use of your gift.

Tools that help

Practice your gift of prayer often. Live in the heart and listen to the heart for the solution of what is needed at the time. Then, in short and precise words, but with a respectful attitude, pray on the behalf of others with acknowledgment, praise and request. Keep it simple; pray in love.

<u>Your Notes</u>:

Chapter 31

Teaching

The gift of teaching is the ability to relay complicated information to others in a manner that is easy for them to understand. This gift requires that you know the material well enough to make it simple to others. The gift of teaching is born when you desire to understand and have epiphanies or deep insights that you want to share with others.

Signs you might have the gift of Teaching:

- You are excited when you learn something new.
- You like to share new information with others.
- When you share information (even a recipe), you do not hold anything back or leave anything out.
- You have an easy grasp of particular subjects and are constantly reading more about these topics.
- You have the ability to experience what you read as you are reading it.
- You have an aptitude for certain subjects and can't learn enough about them.

- You are often self-taught about the subjects that you teach, at least to some degree.
- You study the material until it becomes second nature to you.
- You look for new props that will enhance the students' grasp of the material.
- You are comfortable in the role of teacher.
- You do not take it personally when students reject the subjects you teach.
- You understand that students usually hear information three times before it is fully realized.
- You do not mind the repetitive.
- You are thrilled when you see comprehension on a student's face.
- You ad-lib while you teach and no two classes are ever exactly the same.
- You mentor others.
- The student can become a friend.
- You accept new input from your students and don't hold rigid ideas about the relationship of teacher/student.
- You listen to your students and teach according to their needs.
- You are accessible.
- You impart the truth of the subject to the best of your abilities and knowledge.
- You understand that the information you impart is received according to Universal providence.

The Spiritual Gifts

Mastering your gift

To master the gift of teaching, you must understand the role of both student and teacher and that these roles may at some point be reversed. It is never beneficial to you or the student to rigidly hold to a set of rules that can change depending on the student. It is in wisdom that you understand everyone has something to teach or a message to give. As a master teacher you must become the student when this time comes and listen as an attentive student would.

How this gift is of useful

The gift of teaching allows you to share whatever topics you have mastered with others. It allows you to impart not only true and reliable information but your unique perspective and style. The gift of teaching allows you to accept that you open pathways into understanding; however, the result of the teaching is not in your control. It is Divine providence whether the student becomes enlightened or educated by the material.

The gift of teaching allows you to share in a unique manner and from the heart all that you have to share. It holds nothing back.

Tools that help

Practice, preparation and presentation are the best tools for the gift of teaching. Know your material. Prepare handouts and lists of resources for further study. Look for presentation techniques that enhance education. Be yourself and share from the heart.

###

Thank you for reading. If you enjoyed the information in this book, please leave a few words or sentences as a review on Amazon and Goodreads or other online book sources.

Reviews are very important to all authors. I know they are to me.

For a bonus, keep reading for an excerpt from Chakra Basics: Fundamental of Spiritual Growth.

Your Notes:

Your Notes:

Your Notes:

Excerpt from Chakra Basics – Preface

This book is designed to teach you more about the basic and fundamental uses of chakras, more about yourself, and more about living a conscious life.

If you have chosen this book to further your understanding about Chakras, then you are aware that we are more than what we see in the mirror. We are multi-dimensional beings consisting of Body, Mind, and Spirit (or Soul).

The body is the physical shell for the soul and the mind. It acts from automatic responses signaled by the Mind or Central Nervous System (CNS). For example, as we learn to walk, we put one foot in front of the other until the body acquires the necessary skill and can use muscle memory to walk without thinking about it.

The mind can be classified as the brain or CNS – that part of us that experiences events and catalogues the emotional or thought reactions. The mind is like a computer. Life experiences, as well as the response to that experience, are programmed into the computer. We respond to these life experiences and events with automatic reactions (thoughts and feelings) for most of our lives. Each thought and feeling affects the energy of the chakras.

The spirit or soul is inside the physical shell of our body; however, it accesses the mind and all emotional and physical responses. The spirit is that part of us that has always lived – it has lived before and will continue to live forever. It is eternal. It is pure energy which cannot be destroyed or created; however, it can be affected by negative thought processes which cause disease and pain in the body. When the soul leaves the body, it retains the mind and body memories.

As you read and study about Chakras you will discover how to better integrate the energy of body, mind, and soul into a more productive life-path.

A sound soul lives in a sound mind and body. Soul Eater

Introduction

The simple definition for "chakra" is energy wheel. The word Chakra (pronounced Shock-Ruh) actually comes from Sanskrit (the primary language of Hinduism and Buddhism) and means "wheels" or "turning."

The wheels are constantly turning and supplying energy to our entire being. It is through the chakras that we receive and download Universal wisdom and intelligence which is consistently flowing into us from the source. This connection to the divine is always there but if we pollute our energy with negativity and pessimism the flow of information can become restricted and blocked. When this flow of wisdom is stunted it is because our chakras have become clouded, darkened, or stagnated by the energy of our own negative thoughts and emotions and the negativity of the people around us.

Consider a clear stream that flows unhampered to the ocean. The water is clean and fresh. It flows joyfully along its path every day. One day someone decides to dump their garbage on the banks of this little stream. Then more people dump their garbage there. Eventually the fresh water becomes dirty. Over time, the rains and other natural events push the garbage out into the stream, and it becomes blocked. The fresh, clear water no longer has a free path to the ocean; it has, in effect, become dammed-up with debris and garbage.

The same example can be applied to the chakras. The energy wheels are affected by the thoughts we hold closest, the thoughts we focus on most often, and the thoughts of others who influence us. An old saying that can be applied to the chakras as well as our daily lives is, "If you lay down with dogs you will get up with fleas."

Thoughts become things; choose the good ones. Mike Dooley

It has been designed that we find strength and understanding from these energy vortices. The chakras are our clear and open channel or pathway with the divine. If the chakras be- come damaged or hindered by the garbage and debris of negativity, the pathway becomes like a clogged drain or polluted stream. This book will teach you how to reopen that channel.

A few things to keep in mind:

- Traditional Christian religious beliefs do not teach or encourage the study of chakras; however, Christian doctrine doesn't prohibit their study either.

- When we desire more knowledge and spiritual awareness the chakras begin to play a major role in awakening and fulfilling that desire.

- The chakras are our gift. Unless we unwrap the gift and take it out of the box it remains a mystery; it is unusable. Opening up the box and examining the gift is also insufficient. We must

The Spiritual Gifts

begin to utilize the gift in order to realize its full potential and benefits.

- This book teaches how to use this gift. As we work through each level of the chakras, we grow exponentially compared to a life of only studying texts and doctrines; we open to receive the enlightenment that has been supplied to us.

- Please use the notations and footnotes as referenced. Sometimes they are definitions and sometimes they provide additional insight or information that should be utilized.

- Chakra-work closely resembles self-analysis. As you work with the individual chakra, it will open to you; it opens your understanding and recall of past events and issues associated with that area, whether these issues have been resolved or not.

- The lists of thought patterns, physical indications, and healthy chakras are general and not inclusive – there are many situations that can cause the chakras to become imbalanced and blocked. These sections are merely to help you find the pattern.

- Although there are many chakras throughout the body, this book will expand on the seven major chakras that form a vertical line from the top of your head to the base of the spine.

- You will work with each chakra, one at a time, as you read through the book. At the end, in the last few chapters, you will use all of the information together in new activities. Working through the book as designed will allow you to easily accomplish the activities.

- In essence, you are teaching yourself from the in- formation in this book; it is similar to a correspondence course. I am your instructor through this book, but because I am not physically present as you do the work, I have presented the chakra-work and exercises in a way that you can do it alone if you follow the directions.

- Be sure to have a notebook and pen handy so you can make notes as you read about each chakra.

- Make the practices at the end of the chapters a morning ritual; do them every day.

I have included several blank pages at the end of each chapter for your notes and inspirations as you read. Please utilize them… after all; this is your workbook on chakras. I urge you to put in the effort and time to do the work as it is presented in this book. You will find many self-help tips and suggestions in the chapters. Doing the exercises in the order presented will provide you with a strong foundation for spiritual growth and reconnect you to the power and force of the Chakras – Your connection to Divine Source.

Love and light,

Chariss

Chapter One: The Root Chakra

The first of the seven major chakras discussed in this book is the Root Chakra. The Root Chakra is the color red and signifies the very basics in life. The gemstones most often associated with the root chakra are either the ruby or the garnet. Ruby is said to bring light to dark places and enhance unity. Garnet inspires passion, personal success, stability, and empowerment.

When we think of the root chakra it is helpful to think of the roots of an oak tree that dig deep into the earth to reach the food and sustenance it requires. Like the roots of the tree, the root chakra is concerned with sustenance and the basics of surviving -- food, shelter, and clothing. The work we choose provides the means for these basics so is included in the issues of the root chakra. Although, these are the fundamental concerns we have, the root also plays an active role in our place in family and community.

The root chakra is located at the very lowest part of our torso -- that part of us that touches the earth when we sit on the ground in lotus position[3]. When we work with the root chakra we are directing our attention to the place of our individual beginnings, also called our root beginnings[4].

Our individual beginnings include:

- Our birth family – the original family we were born or adopted into, the beliefs that were passed down to us from our ancestors, and the world view we have gathered from our inheritance and original family

- Our experiences as young children in the birth family and in elementary school; the interactions we had with peers – how we were perceived and how we perceived ourselves in the group setting

- Our birth family's character or reputation and how they were perceived in the extended family and in the com- munity

The root chakra filters and integrates these inherited beliefs and experiences into energy. For example, if our family had the reputation of being hard workers, that belief is held in the root chakra and will fulfill itself in our life, too. If there was abuse in our original family and throughout past generations, that belief is held in the root chakra also. These beliefs are difficult, but not impossible, to overcome because they go back for many generations.

It is critical to understand our beginning so that we can be- gin to see ourselves with love and acceptance. Love and acceptance heals the energy of the chakras. And in love, we better understand ourselves and the purpose of our lives.

Keep in mind that the beliefs handed down to us and held in the root chakra may or may not be true. The root chakra is not concerned about the truthfulness of the beliefs; its purpose is to supply energy to our body systems and work with the information it has been given. It is usually much later in life that we begin to question these inherited beliefs. Questioning our beliefs enables us to correct any negative energy in the root chakra and replace it with positive energy.

Some examples of thought patterns that block the root chakra energy:

- Excessive worry -- about finances, money, or security – this includes job and mortgage security

- Fear – about our physical safety and/or having our basic needs of food, shelter, and clothing met – this also includes the fear of losing what we have

- Obsessions – anything that completely occupies the mind -- this includes refusing to let go of the past and excessive preoccupation with future experiences and thoughts of what if things had been different

- Refusal to accept things as they are – holding onto old ideas, old grievances, and reliving the past; also includes wanting things to be different, daydreaming about how things could or should have been; not living in the present with acceptance

- Trying to please our parents or family at the expense of our own happiness

- Feeling as if we can never get our parent's or family's approval at any price

- Rejecting all ties and communications with other family members

- Cutting-off emotional ties with our roots – family, hometown, high school friends and reunions, and history

- Frequently relocating – this includes the belief that the pasture is greener on the other side

- Rebelling against all family or community teachings – this includes the belief that all of these teachings are bad without having weighed each one with care

Some physical indications that the root chakra energy is blocked:

- Colon and bowel problems – constipation can signify holding onto old ideas or grievances; diarrhea can signify giving up too easily, letting go without considering all the possibilities; and irritable bowel syndrome can indicate vacillating between the two

- Energy flow problems – too little energy keeps us from accomplishing daily tasks or routines; too much energy can prevent us from accomplishing anything because we are bouncing around from idea to idea without the ability to finish anything; and mixed energy or rebounding between having too much and too little energy can suggest vacillating between the two

- Organizational problems -- disorganized and cluttered workspace in home and office environments block energy flow; overflowing closets, hoarding, cluttered kitchen counters, floors, and desks all imply root chakra blockages

- Inability to form lasting relationships

- Gobbling -- this includes eating and drinking too fast, but also refers to devouring relationships with others by using and abusing people then moving on without concern for their welfare

A healthy root chakra allows for the following:

- An adequate diet for strength and energy

- Adequate time for rest and exercise

- A home that is safe, pleasing, and uncluttered

- A love and openness for family and friends

- A tie to community and/or neighborhoods

- A satisfying and rewarding work

- A solid and believable worldview

- An ease and peace with and from life

- The ability to form lasting relationships whether intimate, casual, or professional

- The ability to set and keep an appropriate schedule allowing for work, rest, nourishment, play, and love

We can think of the root chakra as governing our childhood from birth to the approximate age of 10. This is the time when we struggle to learn a delicate balance in order to fit with our original family and to those with whom we are closely associated. At this stage of our development, we want desperately to be accepted as part of the larger group – primarily our family.

We learn by example and by experience what is considered acceptable behavior in most situations. We learn from our parents to have both a public and private face. For example, we learn what we can and cannot do when in public, what our parents will allow us to get away with, and what makes them proud or will embarrass them.

Some of us learned the lessons by way of example and others learned when our parents administered a quick, sharp slap to the bottom or thigh. Still others were taught these lessons by brutal and excessive force. No matter how we learned, these experiences are a large part of our root chakra issues today; they are embedded in our core beliefs.

While we lived and learned in our birth family, we accepted the teachings of our parents as the word of God. How could we not see them in such a manner? The nourishment we received, both emotional and physical, came from them. They were bigger and stronger and we wanted to believe everything they told us even if it didn't make sense; even when our own personal totality -- body, mind, and soul -- disagreed with the things we were taught.

As a young child we saw the world around us with purity and light. Our chakras were open and working near perfectly, especially the third-eye chakra. For example, with a flawlessly working third-eye chakra, we saw our spiritual companions and those of our parents and siblings. We knew they were real but as time passed we discovered that it was more acceptable not to see these beings; that others did not see them. Wanting to fit-in and be agreeable, we stopped seeing with our third-eye.

Another example is the pure and unequivocal joy we felt streaming from our lower chakras[6]. Happiness was total but so was sadness. We expressed ourselves freely and with abandon. We laughed freely. We cried easily. We felt as if we could be or do anything, even fly. We jumped and danced to the warmth of these emotions; we felt no fear. But as part of our training and indoctrination, these gods who watched over us imparted their fears – "don't, you might get hurt, stop". As a result, we became cautious and fearful; we stopped doing and being our truest life-form for fear that something would hurt us or get us.

These were the lessons we learned. This is not to place blame on our parents or caregivers. They only taught us what they knew and the way they had been taught. They only imparted the wisdom of their ancestors. They passed their world view on to us as it had been passed on to them.

As we grew and attended school we had a new set of influences from teachers and peers. We listened and were concerned about what others our own age thought of us. Our first influence outside the home and family was powerful and it added to insights about our personal lives and our reputation and character. For example, it might have been on the school playground that we first discovered what others thought about our family and our status in the community.

This information has become a major part of our belief system and is deeply embedded in our root chakras even now.

Any insecurities, self-doubts, or embarrassments that happened during this young age are surely still with us today. These influences have impacted our adult life in major and minor ways.

Working with our root chakra, we have an opportunity to break the negative cycles that were ingrained in our beginnings. We can reevaluate the beliefs and indoctrination that was passed down from our ancestors. The first step to change is to become aware of the root chakra issues. Now we have an opportunity to remove these influences.

As you work through the exercise below, be open to something different. Working with the root chakra will allow you to boldly declare:

I know where I came from!

NOTE: I recommend that you read the Step One exercise several times to become very familiar with it. You might find it extremely helpful to read the directions into a recording device and play it back during the exercise. We will use Step One as an opener for all the work we do now and in the remaining chapters. In fact, it is an excellent tool to use every day, twice a day. Please do all the steps in each chapter's exercise and in order. Remember that the information discussed in each chakra is intended for the reader. It is not a weapon to be used on family and friends. Please be respectful of others and the path they are on. Don't diagnose others from the lists given in this book.

The Spiritual Gifts

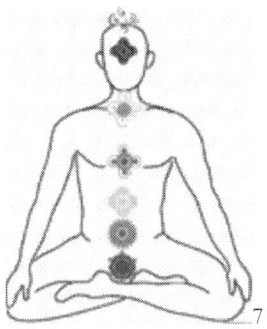

Look at the diagram and focus your attention at the base of the image on the lowest energy wheel which is the root chakra. The root chakra is red, beautiful, and strong. It signifies everything we have just covered in this chapter.

A Root Chakra Exercise:

Step One – Preparation: Balance, Shield-Up, White Light

1. Sit on the floor in the lotus position shown in the diagram. If you are unable to take this position due to physical limitations, the next best choice is to sit on a cushion with ankles crossed. If neither of these options is practical for you, then sit in a chair with your back straight and legs slightly parted.

2. Visualize a white beam of light about four inches in diameter coming down from the Universe and entering the top of your head. The beam of light travels down your spine to the bottom of your tail bone. We will use the term "balance" for this part of the exercise.

3. Next, visualize that this light while staying in the column of your spine also expands into a protective shield around you from the top of your head to the soles of your feet. You are cocooned in

white light. We will use the term "Shield-up" for this part of the exercise.

4.   As you feel the warmth of this energy in your spine and all around you, ask for this same divine substance of white light to fall on you from above like a shower or waterfall. We will use the term "White Light" for this part of the exercise.

Tips:

- When you begin to work with white light it might be helpful to boost your visualization by standing under the shower with the water running directly on the top of your head. This is how the white light enters into your crown chakra.

- When visualizing, eyes can be open or closed.

- When sitting in the lotus position, it is preferable that your root (that place on your body below the perineum) is actually as close as possible to the ground or floor.

Step Two – Root Chakra Work

1.   Find the red root chakra on the image provided for Step One. Now focus your intention on the red energy of your own root chakra. See the white light surrounding it in love, warmth, and acceptance. The white light is healing energy, divine energy.

2.   As you focus on the root chakra, you will be impressed with its color and clarity. Is the red clear and bright or is it dull? Do you notice that the red color is cloudy? Does it have darker shades mixed in

with the red? Is it ruby red, barn red, or candy apple red? Make mental notes of what you sense.

3. If thoughts or memories come to you of childhood look at them closely with love rather than judgment or blame. You may remember a time when you were harmed by an adult or another child. This painful time may have been simply because you belonged to a particular family, church, or organization. You may have been harmed because of who your parents were and it had nothing to do with you. You may remember a time that you harmed someone else. You may remember that your parents harmed you. You may remember a time that you learned you could not depend on your parents to protect you. Do not judge these memories or thoughts. Just look at them; experience them again.

4. After you have spent a few moments revisiting the thoughts or memories, consciously send white light as a blessing to the situations or memories that have come to your attention as you continue to focus on the root chakra.

5. Bless each memory and each event or situation that you are reminded of from the past. Learn to bless everything for "what you bless, blesses you and what you curse, curses you."

6. After blessing each memory or event, let it go.

7. Now, ask the white light to fill the root chakra with healing and love. Take a few moments to feel the warmth and love as it surrounds the root chakra.

8. Spend at least a week on this exercise. When the color of the root chakra is clear and bright, you

are ready to continue to Chapter Two, The Sacral Chakra.

Note: Many times we have experienced a situation or circumstance without feeling it. We were there, our bodies were there, but our minds blocked the feeling or emotional pain. As we look back on the circumstance now it might seem as if it happened to someone else or that it is happening to us for the first time. As the feeling of the situations come back, feel it and experience it. You were much younger then, but now you are older and wiser. You can handle it. Allow yourself to experience it fully now and then simply let it go.

<u>Your Notes:</u>

Your Notes:

Your Notes:

About the Author

Award-winning author, Chariss K. Walker, M.Msc., Reiki Master/Teacher writes both fiction and nonfiction books with a metaphysical and spiritual component. Her fiction expresses a visionary/metaphysical message that illustrates growth in a character's consciousness while utilizing a paranormal aspect. Her nonfiction books share insight, hope, and inspiration. Even though Chariss writes dark-fiction about insanely dark topics, such as sexual abuse, incest, pedophilia, sexual assault, and other inappropriate dinner conversation, there is always an essential question of the abstract nature that gives a reader increasing awareness and perception. All of her books are sold worldwide in eBook, paperback, and many are in large print.
You can learn more about Chariss at her website: www.chariss.com.

Other books by Chariss K. Walker

Fiction Books:

The Vision Chronicles – Paranormal Metaphysical Thrillers
Kaleidoscope, Book 1
Spyglass, Book 2
Window's Pane, Book 3
Windows All Around, Book 4
Open Spaces, Book 5
Stream of Light, Book 6
Lamp's Light, Book 7
Clear Glass, Book 8
A Dream Come True: A Novelette for The Vision Chronicles series, Book 9

The Retreat
The Journey

Becky Tibbs: A North Carolina Medium's Mystery Series:
A Medium's Birthday Surprise, Book 1
A Medium's Thanksgiving Table, Book 2
A Medium's Christmas Gift, Book 3
A Medium's Valentine's Day Delight, Book 4
A Medium's Easter Epiphany, Book 5

Dark Fiction Books:

An Alec Winters Series – Dark Supernatural Suspense/Urban Fantasy:
Prelude, Book 1
Crescent City, Book 2
Port City, Book 3
Harbor City, Book 4

Serena McKay Novels - Dystopian Crime Female P.I. Thrillers
Purple Kitty, Book 1
Blue Cadillac, Book 2
my name is tookie

Nonfiction Books:

A Beginner's Guide to Visualization
Chakra Basics
The Spiritual Gifts
Abundance
Many Paths to Healing
Keep the Faith
Make a Joyful Noise
Make a Joyful Noise Study Guide
Finding Serenity 3-Book Boxed-Set
Going Deeper 6-Book Series:
A Beginner's Guide to Releasing Trapped Emotions, #1
Release Chakra Trapped Emotions, #2
Release Common Disease Trapped Emotions, #3
Release Hindrances to Success, #4

Chariss K. Walker

Release Body Systems Trapped Emotions, #5
Release Mental Blocks, #6
Letting go of Pain

I really appreciate you reading my book! Please take a moment to leave a review. A few words or sentences will do because reviews are very important to every author and to other readers. I know reviews are important to me. Be sure to connect with me on Amazon, Goodreads, Facebook, Twitter, and BookBub.

Additional Resources

The following lists additional resources that you might find helpful. Due to the dynamic nature of the internet, if web addresses are listed, it is not possible to guarantee that they have not changed or that they still exist. In this case, use the key words of the link to perform your own Internet search.

The resources provided below are samples that will assist you in your search for understanding. The author has given only a few to get you, the reader, started. Let them be a guide as you seek understanding…

Teaching Resources

Testing Human Energy –

http://youtu.be/xC60tyDpWFs

Muscle Testing & Applied Kinesiology Demonstration -- http://youtu.be/iWNsh-Yh32E

Working with Ki, Chi or Soul Energy – http://youtu.be/Zhjq45-0khc

Recommended Reading

You Can Heal Your Life, Louise Hay

Infinite Possibilities, Mike Dooley

Siddhartha, Hermann Hesse

Transition Now: Redefining Duality, Lee Carroll, et al

Manufactured by Amazon.ca
Bolton, ON